perfect
preserves

perfect
preserves

Hilaire Walden

Jelly-making

Canning

Pickling

Smoking Curing

Potting Freezing

Salting

Crystalizing

Drying

Wiley Publishing, Inc.

A QUINTET BOOK

Published by Wiley Publishing, Inc., New York, NY

Copyright © Quintet Publishing Limited, 2002

ISBN   0-7645-6705-5

Contact the Library of Congress for complete Cataloging-in-Publication Data.

This book was designed and produced by
Quintet Publishing Limited
6 Blundell Street
London N7 9BH

Project Editor: Anna Southgate
Editor: Erin Connell
Art Direction and Design: Simon Daley
Photography: Ian Bagwell
Food Styling: Kathryn Hawkins and Jacqueline Bellefontaine

Managing Editor: Diana Steedman
Creative Director: Richard Dewing
Publisher: Oliver Salzmann

First Edition
10 9 8 7 6 5 4 3 2 1

Manufactured in Singapore by Universal Graphics Pte Ltd
Printed in China by Leefung-Asco Printers Trading Ltd

Contents

Introduction

Nowadays, most foods are readily available year-round, and because of refrigeration, there seems to be no need to preserve foods at times of glut for use later when they are scarce. But preserving, like bread making and baking, appeals to the inner self: it's therapeutic, rewarding, and fun. And everyone loves the taste of homemade preserved foods, whether it is a jam or chutney, a country pâté, or apricots bottled with vanilla.

Making your own preserves makes sense in so many ways. Homemade preserves based on good recipes are of a higher quality and are more economical than their mass-produced, commercial counterparts. This is especially true if preserving is done using produce from your own garden, with home-grown fruits and vegetables from friends or family who frequently have a surplus, or if you have access to wild foods that are known to be safe to eat. If you do not grow your own fruits and vegetables, there is a growing number of pick-your-own farms and orchards, as well as farmers' markets, where you can buy quality produce at reasonable prices when the food is at its freshest. When you make your own preserves, you know exactly how they have been made and what has been used to make them, so you can be assured that they are free from preservatives, colors, and other additives.

When you are overwhelmed with plums from your yard, or find it hard to resist the wonderful, inexpensive tomatoes that you see for sale at a farm stand, turn to the following pages to find how to make the best use of them. If you buy a side of pork, for example, turn some of it into rillettes (see page 154) or make your own pâté (see page 157). Extend the shelf life of some of the whole salmon you have been given, or have caught, by making gravlax (see page 150).

Preserving gives you an enormous outlet for using your imagination. As with other types of cooking, after first making the tried-and-tested recipes found in this book, you can adapt them and add your own personal touches. Change the flavors to reflect your own choices, or to suit the tastes of friends if you are going to give the preserve as a present. For an Asian flavor, use spices such as cardamom, Szechuan peppercorns, lemon grass, and cumin. Add rose water or vanilla beans to strawberry or raspberry preserves. Or, instead of using traditional raisins, add dried figs, apricots, peaches, pears, cranberries, or cherries; you can even try some of the exotic dried fruits that are now readily available, such as mango, papaya, and banana. If you find commercially made chutneys and pickles too harsh, you will find the homemade versions far more accessible because they are made with mellow wine vinegars. The amount of sugar can be lowered slightly to make your preserves less sweet, or increased for a sweeter taste. If you love garlic, add some chopped cloves; if hot food is a favorite, pop in some chiles. It doesn't take long to build up your own repertoire of personal recipes.

Contrary to what many people believe, preserving can be done without complicated, costly equipment, and most people already have what they need right in their kitchen. For example, a special preserving pan is not necessary unless you are making preserves in large quantities. Preserving isn't a skill or art, and in the following pages, you will find all the essential information, as well as the model methods, to guide you safely and successfully through the making of preserves.

With a stock of your own preserves on the shelves, you will always be able to make an interesting, simple, and quick meal — whether it's perking up a straightforward cheese sandwich or plate of cold meats, or enlivening cooked dishes. You will discover many good examples throughout the book.

Homemade preserves are ideal for giving because they are truly personal gifts, satisfying to both receiver and giver. So, if you keep a selection of preserves in the cupboard, you will never be at a loss for a present if you've forgotten a birthday, or are unexpectedly asked to donate something to a school fundraiser, or if you run out of gift-giving ideas during the winter holidays.

Equipment

Equipment used for making preserves containing fruit or vinegar must be made of a nonreactive material, such as stainless steel, plastic, nylon, or wood. It is also important to remember to use heatproof utensils for hot preserves.

Pans A traditional preserving pan, called a maslin, has sloping sides, a lip for pouring, and a carrying handle. It is useful, especially when making large quantities of preserves, but it is not essential. The pan you use should have the following characteristics:

■ It should be made of a nonreactive material, such as stainless steel, or have a nonstick or enamel lining. Unlined copper or brass pans, or anything made of aluminum, should not be used.
■ It should be heavy and have a thick, flat bottom so that heat is conducted evenly and mixtures do not catch and burn.
■ If possible, it should have sides that slope outwards to provide a large surface area to allow for the rapid evaporation of surplus liquid and steam. If boiling a fairly small quantity of a sauce or syrup, a large, nonstick frying pan or a nonreactive saucepan can be used instead.
■ It should have an inner surface free of blemishes, pitting, or damage.
■ It should have two handles opposite each other to make for easier lifting.
■ It should not be more than half-full when cooking sweetened mixtures, as they can spit and splutter when boiled.

Scales A scale is not necessary for making preserves, but it can be very helpful. Try to accurately note the weight of ingredients prior to purchase. To weigh large amounts of ingredients at home, a bathroom scale can be used. Put the pan, or another large container, on the scale, re-set to zero, and add the ingredients. Alternatively, note the weight of the empty pan, add the ingredients, and deduct the pan's weight from the total.

Knives Using sharp, stainless steel knives of good quality can prevent the discoloration of fruit and vegetables and will ensure quick, easy, neat, and safe preparation.

Spice bag This small bag is usually made of cheesecloth or muslin and has a drawstring top. It can be purchased, or it can be improvised at home using a small piece of cheesecloth tied at the top with a long piece of string. The bag is tied to the handle of the pan and is suspended in the preserves to impart flavor. Metal spice balls that clip onto the side of the pan can also be used.

Long-handled wooden spoon A wooden spoon with a long handle keeps your hands away from very hot liquids, steam, and "spitting" mixtures. Wood is essential because metal may react with the acid present and discolor the ingredients.

Slotted spoon During boiling, jams and jellies frequently produce scum, which must be removed to keep the finished preserves from turning cloudy. A slotted spoon is also useful for scooping out the pits of fruits such as plums and peaches.

Candy thermometer A candy thermometer clips to the side of the pan and allows the temperature of jams, jellies, and marmalades to be easily read, ensuring that the preserves reach the correct setting point (see Model Methods for specific temperatures, page 20). If using a free-standing thermometer, hold it in the center of the preserve mixture for a minute or so before reading it.

Sieves and colanders These should be made of nylon or plastic.

Bowls A selection of bowls of various sizes is essential.

Measuring cup A heatproof measuring cup is necessary for measuring and pouring hot liquids.

Funnel Two funnels, one a wide-mouthed funnel for filling jars, and a narrow one for filling bottles, are handy, and should ideally have a nonstick surface. This facilitates the clean transfer of hot liquids or preserves from one container to another.

Ladle This is used for transferring preserves from the pan to pour through the funnel.

Jelly bag and stand A jelly bag, available for purchase at stores that carry a wide variety of home canning supplies, is a bag made of a finely woven material, usually nylon. It is very inexpensive to buy and can be washed and reused. It is chiefly used when making jellies to facilitate the extraction of juice from the ingredients being used, and is suspended over a bowl to catch the drips of liquid. Some jelly bags are supplied with their own stand, but one can easily be improvised by attaching the bag to a wire coat hanger and hanging from a hook. A homemade jelly bag can be created using two or three layers of cheesecloth or fine cotton. A jelly bag should always be scalded shortly before it is used.

Pressure cooker When a recipe calls for precooking the ingredients, this can be used to save time and help retain the color and flavor during the preliminary softening of the fruit, peel, or vegetables. Consult the manufacturer's handbook for recipes and timings.

Boiling-water canner Boiling-water canners are recommended by the United States Department of Agriculture (USDA) for heat-treating jams, jellies, butters, cheeses, marmalades, chutneys, pickles, and some fruits.

These canners are made of aluminum or porcelain-covered steel and have removable perforated racks and fitted lids. A canner must be deep enough so that the jars are covered by at least 1 inch of briskly bubbling water during processing. If you use an electric stove, the canner must have a flat bottom, and should be no more than 4 inches wider than the element on which it will be heated.

Jars and bottles Wide-mouthed jars with openings of about 3 inches are the most useful for pickles because they are easier to fill. For jams, jellies, and marmalades 2$\frac{1}{2}$-inch mouthed jars can be used. The best sizes to use for home-canning are 2 cup and 1 quart. If they are handled and used carefully they can be reused several times if new lids are used each time.

These jars must be inspected carefully to make sure they are free of cracks, chips, or other flaws. If a hot mixture is added to a flawed jar, the jar will immediately shatter. Bacteria can breed in small cracks or chips, which could cause the preserve to spoil.

To sterilize jars and bottles before using them, first wash well in hot, soapy water, then rinse in hot water. Put them, open-side up, in a deep pan, cover with boiling water, and boil rapidly for 10 minutes. Lift them out with tongs and leave to drain upside down on a thick dish towel. Washing in the dishwasher is not recommended.

Use warm jars when filling with hot preserves to prevent cracking, but leave them to cool when filling with cold preserves.

Always use a container that is appropriate for the amount of preserve so that it is filled to the optimum level (see individual methods).

Covers and lids Acid-proof screw-top or snap-on lids, or those that have an acid-proof lining (such as plastic) can also be used for the final covering for sweet preserves, while they must be vinegar-proof or have a vinegar-proof lining for chutneys and pickles and other vinegar-containing preserves. If you do only have metal lids, cover the top of the jar with cling film before putting on the lid.

For boiling-water canning (see page 14), use two-part lids that are specifically designed for this purpose. The lids have a special seal and cannot be reused; they are held in place by metal screw-bands. The screw-bands and the jars, however, can be recycled. For instructions on how to properly seal the jars, consult the manufacturer's directions. The most usual type of self-sealing lid consists of a flat metal lid with a metal screw band to hold it in place during processing. The lid has a crimped bottom edge that forms a trough, which is filled with a colored gasket compound. When the jars are processed the lid gasket softens and flows slightly to cover the jar-sealing surface, yet allows air to escape from the jar. The gasket then forms an airtight seal as the jar cools. Inspect lids carefully before they are used to ensure they are free of defects and that the compound is perfect.

Do not keep lids from year to year because the quality of the compound deteriorates with time. These self-sealing lids have a five-year shelf life and it is advisable to buy only the quantity you need each time. When two-part lids are used for boiling-water canning, follow the manufacturer's directions for preparing them. In general, the lids and screw-tops should be washed in hot, soapy water and rinsed with hot water. The screw-tops can be placed on a dish towel to dry; the lids should be placed in a pan, covered with water, and brought to a simmer, but not boiled, and kept warm.

Ingredients

Sugar When making preserves, fruit must always be cooked before sugar is added to it or the fruit will harden and no amount of cooking will tenderize it. This hardening can be used deliberately if, for example, you want soft fruit such as strawberries and raspberries to remain whole; sprinkle them with sugar and leave overnight before cooking.

Granulated sugar, or "regular" sugar, is the sweetener that is most widely used for making preserves. It is usually warmed in a heatproof bowl in a low oven for about 20 minutes before use to hasten the dissolving in the liquid.

A specialty sugar, called preserving sugar, can also be used for making jams, jellies, and marmalades. It has a larger crystal structure than granulated sugar and, when used, forms less scum and produces slightly brighter, clearer results. Jam sugar is another specialty sugar, and is a mixture of sugar and pectin. It is particularly useful when making jams and jellies with low-pectin fruits because it reduces the boiling to set time to about four minutes, thus giving a better flavor and a clear, bright color. Both preserving sugar and jam sugar may be difficult to find, as they are not readily available in the United States. They can be ordered online through www.whitworths-sugars.com.

Brown sugar, both light and dark, is mostly used for savory preserves such as chutneys and pickles.

Changing the type of sugar in a preserve will alter the flavor, and is not recommended unless specified in the recipe.

Pectin The presence of pectin is vital if a jam, jelly, or marmalade is to set. Pectin is a natural, gum-like substance found in the cells of fruit. It is extracted from the fruit during cooking, and with the right combination of acid (present in the fruit, or added in the form of lemon juice) and sugar, it produces a set.

Under-ripe fruit has a higher level of pectin than ripe fruit. Fruits vary in the amounts of pectin they contain. Fruits that are low in pectin are usually combined with a high-pectin fruit, or lemon juice; commercial pectin (in powder or liquid form) or jam sugar (sugar with pectin) can also be used.

Acid Acid must be present for jams and jellies to set. It may be present in the fruit, or it can be added in the form of lemon juice or citric acid. The acid content of fruit declines as it ripens, which is why slightly under-ripe fruit should be used for preserves that need to set. Strawberries, sweet apples, pears, cherries, and ripe, late-season blackberries need additional acid: allow 2 tablespoons lemon juice or $\frac{1}{2}$ teaspoon citric acid to 4 pounds low-pectin fruit.

Salt If possible, kosher salt, sea salt, or pickling salt should be used instead of table salt (except for brining). There are additives in table salt that can cause discoloration and may inhibit some preservative qualities.

Vinegar While any vinegar can be used, I prefer white or red wine vinegars because they have a subtle flavor that doesn't compete with the food being preserved. Asian rice vinegars are even milder than wine vinegars, but some have a level of acetic acid that is lower than five percent, the level necessary for making preserves that can be kept without refrigeration. Cider vinegar can be used for a more fruity taste.

Spices Always try to use freshly purchased spices. If you like, toast the spice in a dry, heavy-bottomed pan over moderately low heat until fragrant, and then lightly crush. This step is not necessary, but it helps to release more of the flavor contained in the spices.

Choosing fruits and vegetables

Fruit and vegetable preserves will have the finest flavor when made with produce that has been grown in its true season and ripened in natural sunlight and warmth. This is particularly important for fruits, bell peppers, eggplants, zucchini, and tomatoes. Because flavor begins to deteriorate soon after harvesting, I recommend using produce as soon as possible after it has been picked, which usually means buying locally grown fruits and vegetables, or using what you have grown in your own garden.

Fruit that is slightly underripe is ideal for jams, jellies, and canning because the pectin content is at its highest (see page 14). Although produce sold by supermarkets is invariably underripe, it is not always best for making preserves. Often, it is picked when it is too underripe (done so it will last longer during shipping) and will not have had time to develop much flavor. In addition, any subsequent ripening may take place in artificial conditions.

If you have fruit that is fully ripe, or if you have a fruit that is low in pectin, don't rule it out for using in jams and jellies; simply add commercial pectin or extra lemon juice. Fully ripe fruit, or fruit that is less than perfect, is excellent for use in curds, fruit butters, fruit cheeses,

syrups, and chutneys, as well as for drying and freezing.

The time of year when a fruit or vegetable comes into season is also the time when it will be most abundant. It will usually be sold at a very reasonable price, which is just the time to snap it up for making batches of preserves. A low price in several retail outlets at the same time is usually a good indication of seasonality.

Seasons obviously vary around the world. For example, in Britain, our tomatoes and peppers do not come fully into their own until late August and September, but in warmer places like Southern France, Italy, or Spain, good supplies of tasty tomatoes and peppers are available earlier in the growing year.

The fruit year in the United States is led by rhubarb

(although really a vegetable, it is considered a fruit), with a season from January to June. Fruits available in late spring through summer include strawberries, cherries, raspberries, blueberries, red currants, and black currants. Plums, pears, and apples have their true season toward the end of the summer through fall. To know what is in season in your area, keep an eye on the local produce stores and farmers' markets.

Fruits and vegetables do not always retain their color when preserved. For example, eggplant skin turns from a rich, dark purple to brown. Another example is kiwi fruit. If you want to have a vibrant green preserve made from kiwi fruit, you will have to freeze them first.

Pectin content of fruit

High Blackberries (mature but unripe), tart cooking apples, crab apples, cranberries, damson plums, gooseberries, lemons, limes, oranges, quinces, and red currants.
Medium Sweet apples, apricots, blackberries (ripe), loganberries, mulberries, plums, raspberries.
Low Bananas, blueberries, cherries, figs, grapes, guavas, japonicas, mangoes, melons, nectarines, peaches, pineapples, rhubarb, strawberries.

Sealing methods

The USDA recommends that a number of preserves should be heat-processed in a boiling-water canner immediately after the preserve has been filled into the jars.

Sealing jams, jellies, marmalades, butters, cheeses, and chutneys in a boiling-water canner

1 Pour water into the canner so that it is half-filled and heat to 180°F.

2 Use jars and lids that are suitable for canning (see page 11). Sterilize and warm them.

3 Fill the hot preserve into the jars to ¼ inch of the top.

4 Insert a flat plastic (not metal) spatula between the preserve and jar to release air bubbles. Slowly turn the jar and move the spatula up and down to allow air bubbles to escape.

5 Using a clean, warm, damp cloth or kitchen paper wipe any preserve from the rim of the jar.

6 Place the lid, gasket down, on the jar then secure with the metal screw band. Follow the manufacturer's instructions for tightening the lids correctly.

7 Place the jars into the canner rack and, using the handles, lower it into the canner. Alternatively, use a jar lifter to load the jars into the canner one at a time.

8 If necessary add boiling water to the canner so that the jars are covered by at least 1 inch.

9 Raise the heat below the canner to its highest setting and bring the water to a vigorous boil. Set a timer for 5 minutes.

10 Fit the canner lid and lower the heat to maintain a steady boil; check it regularly as well as the level of the water, adding more if necessary.

11 At the end of the processing time, remove the canner from the heat and remove the lid. Using a jar lifter, transfer the jars to a towel or cooling rack, leaving at least 1 inch between each jar. Leave to cool, upright, for 12 to 24 hours. Do not retighten the lids.

12 Once the jars have cooled, test for a tight seal. The screw bands can now be removed, washed, dried and stored in a dry place for re-use.

13 Label and date the jars and store in a clean, cool, dark, dry place.

Canning fruit in a boiling-water canner

1 Pour water into the canner so that it is half-filled and heat to 180°F.

2 Fill the fruit and syrup into the jars to within ¼ inch of the top.

3 Fit the lids (see page 14) and screw bands then put into the canner rack and, using the handles, lower it into the canner. Alternatively, use a jar lifter to load the jars into the canner one at a time.

4 If necessary add boiling water to the canner so that the jars are covered by at least 1 inch.

5 Raise the heat below the canner to its highest setting and bring the water to a vigorous boil. Set a timer for the required time (see right).

6 Proceed as above.

NOTE The USDA also recommends that fermented pickles such as sauerkraut, should be heat-processed in a boiling water canner. No such pickles have been included in this book.

Processing times for fruit canned in a boiling-water canner*

FRUIT	QUANTITY	TIME (MINUTES)
Apple butter	2 cup	5
	4 cup	10
Apples, sliced	2 cup	20
	4 cup	20
Apricots	2 cup	20
	4 cup	25
Berries	2 cup	15
	4 cup	15
Cherries	2 cup	15
	4 cup	20
Figs	2 cup	15
	4 cup	15
Nectarines/peaches, sliced halved	2 cup	20
	4 cup	25
Pears, halved	2 cup	20
	4 cup	25
Pineapple	2 cup	15
	4 cup	20
Plums	2 cup	20
	4 cup	25
Rhubarb, stewed	2 cup	15
	4 cup	15

Processing times for purees, sauces and syrups*

QUANTITY	TIME (MINUTES)
2½-cup bottles	20
4⅓-cup bottles	25
(Hot fill from time water reaches simmering)	

* At 0 to 1,000 feet above sea level. For altitudes above 1,000 feet above sea level, adjust the processing times according to the following table.

1,001 to 3,000 ft above sea level	add 5 minutes
3.001 to 6,000 ft above sea level	add 10 minutes
6,001 to 8,000 ft above sea level	add 15 minutes
8,001 to 10,000 ft above sea level	add 20 minutes

Storage

Preserves should be kept in a cool, dark, dry place, preferably between 50 and 70°F; this used to be an old-fashioned larder, which would be on the coolest wall, such as a north- or east-facing wall, so that it always remained cool inside.

But nowadays, not only do houses rarely have larders but they are also maintained at higher temperatures, thanks to central heating. So, if your house, and therefore your kitchen, is very warm (unless specifically directed to keep a preserve in the fridge) you should store your unopened preserves either somewhere other than the kitchen, such as in a box in a bedroom that is kept cooler than the rest of the house, or perhaps in the garage. Once opened, keep the preserves in a refrigerator. Sweet preserves like jams, jellies, marmalades, butters and cheeses, should be kept cooler than high-acid foods, such as chutneys and pickles, especially after they have been opened.

All preserves will improve if kept for a while before being eaten, even if only for a day or so in the case of a fruit curd. But the majority should be stored for at least one month, some much longer. For optimum quality, eat preserves within a year. After this time chemical changes start to occur which may affect the color, flavor and/or nutrition of the food. See individual recipes for times and any special conditions.

Ensure all preserves are adequately sealed before storing, and check them regularly for any signs of deterioration. Discard any that are fermenting or smell unpleasant, or if the seal has broken on a bottled preserve.

Hygiene

Cleanliness and coolness when making preserves are vitally important because warmth and moisture encourage bacterial growth. Therefore work in a well-ventilated kitchen that is kept as cool as possible.

Wash your hands before starting a project, or as soon as they become a little soiled, and dry them on a clean towel. If your hands become hot, wash them under a running cold tap.

All the equipment you use should be spotlessly clean and washed frequently in hot, soapy water, or a dishwasher, and, if possible, left to dry naturally. Particular care must be taken when preparing meat

and fish: if they are kept in a fridge before they are used, the fridge must be maintained at below 40°F; the kitchen should ideally be at no more than 54°F; and separate, scrupulously clean, equipment, including chopping boards, must be used and washed-up immediately after use.

Use disposable cloths or kitchen paper for wiping surfaces, throwing them away after each use.

Presenting preserves

A gift of homemade preserves is special in and of itself, but it can very easily be made into something extra special with a little effort and without much skill or added expense.

■ Use safe, interestingly-shaped jars, bottles, and pots, such as: angular-sided and straight-sided jars; no-shoulder jars; tall and slim jars; or short and squat, flask-style jars. Keep handy a range of sizes as well, so that you can make multi-packs of a number of different preserves. Decorative bottles and preserving jars can be bought quite inexpensively from kitchenware, homestore, and hardware shops.

■ Fix a stencil on the bottle or jar, cover all other parts of the container and surrounding surfaces, and spray the stencil with metallic paint to simulate an etched effect.

■ Paint the bottle or jar with glass paint, or highlight the design that is already on the container.

■ Affix neatly cut-out shapes of appropriate objects, such as oranges for a jar of marmalade, to the bottles. Cover the back of the shape with adhesive, position on the container, and press in place. Let dry.

■ All preserves must be properly sealed, but the container tops can be made more attractive by adding covers made of fabric. Choose a design to suit the recipient or the message you wish to convey. Some

suggestions are: a cheerfully patterned fabric; a plain, sophisticated material; a country-style fabric; or even an elegant fabric like silk. Metallic crepe paper and brightly colored waxed paper can also be used.

■ Cut the cover with pinking shears for a decorative edge, or sew around the edge with a blanket or scallop stitch. Tie it on with a pretty contrasting or complementing ribbon, or string.

■ Design and make hand-painted labels, writing on them with crayon, gold or silver marker, or highlighter. Laundry markers can be used directly on fabric. Tags can also be made from a shiny, colorful, foil-backed card. Include not only the name of the preserve, but also the date when it was made, the "eat by" date, and any special notes, such as interesting ways to use the preserve or any history behind it.

■ Use attractive fabric ribbon to attach the labels and tags. Curling ribbon or foil ribbon can be stretched over a scissor blade to curl into ringlets.

■ Combine an appropriate serving spoon, or a saucer on which to stand the preserve, in your gift.

1 Model methods

Making jam

When making jam, the amount of sugar that is added varies according to the sugar content of the fruit, but it normally accounts for 60 to 65 percent of the weight of the finished jam. The longer the jam is cooked, the more water that will be needed.

EQUIPMENT

Sterilized jars
(see page 11)

Heatproof bowl

Small plate or saucer

Sharp stainless steel
knife (optional)

Cutting board

Large, nonreactive pan

Long-handled wooden
spoon

Candy thermometer
(optional)

Teaspoon

Baking sheet or
wooden board

Slotted spoon

Heatproof ladle

Flat plastic spatula

Clean dishcloth and
hot soapy water

Boiling-water canner

Labels

INGREDIENTS

Sugar

Slightly underripe,
blemish-free fruit,
unwashed for
preference

Lemon juice (optional)

Pat of unsalted butter
(optional)

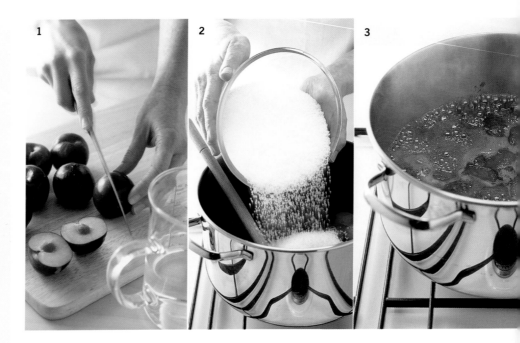

1 Put the jars in a low oven to keep warm. Put the sugar into a bowl and place in the oven as well, and put the plate or saucer in the refrigerator. Make sure the fruit is clean and free of blemishes, and prepare according to type. Put the fruit in the pan with the specified amount of water and heat.

2 Remove the pan from the heat and pour in the warm sugar. Then, heat gently, stirring with a wooden spoon, until the sugar has dissolved. A pat of butter can be added after the sugar to reduce the formation of scum.

3 Increase the heat and boil rapidly, without stirring, until the setting point is reached. This should take between 10 and 15 minutes. The correct temperature should be 220°F on the candy thermometer.

5 Skim any scum from the surface of the jam using a slotted spoon. Leave the jam to stand for about 10 minutes before filling the jars so the fruit is evenly distributed throughout and does not rise to the top of the jars. Prepare and fill the jars (see page 11), then heat-process in a boiling-water canner. (See page 14).

5

4 To test for a set without a thermometer, remove the pan from the heat and try either one of these methods. Drop a little of the jam onto the cold saucer and push it gently with a teaspoon or your fingertip. If the surface wrinkles, the setting point has been reached. Or, lift some of the jam from the pan on the wooden spoon, let it cool slightly, and then allow it to drip back into the pan. If the drops run together along the edge of the spoon and form one unified flake, or sheet, which breaks off sharply as it falls back into the pan, the jam is ready.

Making jellies

The basic method and principles of making jelly are much the same for jam, but there are some extra points to watch for, and more time is needed. High-pectin fruits (see page 14) make the best jellies, although low-pectin fruits can be used if combined with other fruits that have a higher pectin content, or if jam sugar (sugar with pectin) is used.

EQUIPMENT

Sterilized jars
  (see page 11)
Heatproof bowl
Small plate or saucer
Sharp stainless steel
  knife (optional)
Cutting board
Large nonreactive pan
Long-handled wooden
  spoon
Jelly bag, or triple
  thickness of cheesecloth
Upturned stool for
  supporting the jelly bag
Large nonreactive bowl
Candy thermometer
  (optional)
Teaspoon
Slotted spoon
Baking sheet or wooden
  board
Heatproof ladle
Flat plastic spatula
Clean dishcloth and hot
  soapy water
Boiling-water canner
Labels

INGREDIENTS

Sugar
Slightly underripe fruit
Water

1 Put the jars in a low oven to keep warm. Put the sugar into a bowl and place in the oven as well, and put the plate or saucer in the refrigerator. Make sure the fruit is clean and that any blemishes have been completely cut out. Prepare the fruit according to type; there is no need to remove the peel, core, and seeds. Put the fruit in the pan with the specified amount of water and simmer gently until the fruit is soft, stirring occasionally with the wooden spoon to prevent sticking.

2 Pour boiling water through the jelly bag or cheesecloth to scald it. Tie the bag to a stand and put the large bowl underneath. Pour the contents of the pan into the bag and leave it to drip in a cool place, undisturbed, for 8 to 12 hours until no more liquid is coming through.

3 Measure the juice in the bowl and return it to a clean pan. Add 2 cups warmed sugar for every 2½ cups juice. Heat gently, stirring with a wooden spoon, until the sugar has dissolved, then raise the heat and boil rapidly until the temperature reaches 220°F on a candy thermometer. Alternatively, use the setting point test (see page 23). Avoid stirring unless necessary, as it can cause air bubbles.

3

4 With the pan off the heat, skim any scum from the surface with a slotted spoon. If the jelly contains particles such as herbs, let it stand for 10 minutes before filling the jars so the particles are evenly distributed throughout the jelly.

5 Prepare and fill the jars (see page 11), then heat-process in a boiling-water canner. (See page 14).

Making marmalade

Marmalades used to be made from a variety of different fruits, but nowadays they almost always contain citrus fruits – either as the only fruit or with another fruit added. The main difference between making jam and marmalade is that the citrus peel must be cooked first, without sugar, to tenderize it and extract the pectin.

EQUIPMENT

Sharp stainless steel knife (optional)
Cutting board
Lemon juicer
Small piece of cheesecloth or spice bag
Kitchen string
Sterilized jars (see page 11)
Small plate or saucer
Large, nonreactive pan
Long-handled wooden spoon
Candy thermometer (optional)
Teaspoon
Slotted spoon
Baking sheet or wooden board
Heatproof ladle
Flat plastic spatula
Clean dishcloth and hot soapy water
Boiling-water canner
Labels

INGREDIENTS

Fruit
Water
Sugar

1 Cut the fruit in half and squeeze out the juice; reserve the seeds and any membrane that comes away during squeezing. Put the seeds and membrane on a piece of cheesecloth and tie into a bag with a long length of string.

2 Slice the citrus peel to the thickness you desire and put into the pan with the citrus juices and the required amount of water. Tie the end of the string to the handle of the pan so it is suspended in the contents. Heat until boiling, then lower the heat and simmer for one to one and a half hours until the peel is soft and the liquid is well reduced.

3

4

3 Put the jars to warm in a low oven to keep warm, and put the small plate or saucer in the refrigerator. Off the heat, remove the cheesecloth bag from the pan and squeeze it hard against the side of the pan to extract the juices. Discard the bag.

4 Add the sugar and heat gently, stirring with a wooden spoon, until it has dissolved. Then, increase the heat and boil hard for 10 to 15 minutes, stirring as necessary, until the setting point is reached (see page 23). The temperature should reach 220°F on a candy thermometer.

5 With the pan off the heat, skim any scum from the surface with a slotted spoon. Let the marmalade stand for 10 minutes. Prepare andfill the jars (see page 11), then heat-process in a boiling-water canner. (See page 14).

Making fruit curds

Made with eggs and butter as well as sugar, curds are not true preserves, and must be kept in the refrigerator, for no more than two to three weeks. It is therefore best to make them in small quantities.

EQUIPMENT

Sterilized jars or pots
  (see page 11)
Saucepan
Heatproof bowl
Wooden spoon
Sieve
Baking sheet or
  wooden board
Heatproof ladle
Nonreactive funnel or
  measuring cup
Clean dishcloth and
  hot soapy water
Labels

INGREDIENTS

Water
Fruit
Unsalted butter, diced
Superfine sugar
Eggs

1 Put the jars or pots in a low oven to keep warm. Heat a saucepan of water to just below the simmering point. Put the fruit, butter, and sugar in a heatproof bowl that will sit over the saucepan without the bottom of the bowl touching the water. Heat the ingredients, stirring occasionally with a wooden spoon, until the butter has melted and the sugar has dissolved.

2 Beat the eggs and strain to remove white "thread." Pour into the bowl, stirring to incorporate them evenly. Continue to heat very gently for 25 to 45 minutes, stirring frequently at first, and then constantly until the mixture is thick enough to coat the back of the spoon. Do not allow it to boil or it will curdle.

3 Prepare the jars (see page 11) and fill. Cover with secure-fitting lids and refrigerate.

NOTE The temperature reached during making a fruit curd is not high enough to cook the eggs thoroughly. Therefore, pregnant women, young children, the elderly, or anyone with an impaired immune system should avoid eating fruit curds.

Making fruit butters and cheeses

Fruit butters and cheeses are made the same way – by cooking fruit puree with sugar until thick. Fruit butters have a soft, butter-like, spreadable consistency. Fruit cheeses are cooked longer, until they are so thick that, when cold, they can be unmolded and cut with a knife, hence the name "cheese." They can also be stored longer than fruit butters. It is only worth making fruit butters and cheeses when there is a glut of fruit, because a large quantity of fruit produces only a comparatively small amount of preserve.

EQUIPMENT

Sterilized jars or pots (see page 11)

Sharp stainless steel knife

Cutting board

Nonreactive pan

Wooden spoon

Nonreactive sieve

Baking sheet or wooden board

Heatproof measuring cup, or ladle

Clean dishcloth and hot soapy water

Boiling-water canner

Labels

INGREDIENTS

Fruit

Water

Superfine sugar

1 Put the jars or pots in a low oven to keep warm. Ripe, over-ripe, or imperfect fruit can be used, providing any blemishes are cut out. Chop fruit into large pieces. Put the fruit in the pan with enough water to cover. Bring to a boil, then simmer until the fruit is very tender and pulpy.

2 Pass the fruit pulp through a sieve, and measure it in the measuring cup to calculate the amount of sugar that will be needed. For a fruit butter, allow 1 to $1\frac{2}{3}$ cups sugar for each $2\frac{1}{2}$ cups puree; for a fruit cheese, allow $2\frac{1}{4}$ cups sugar for each $2\frac{1}{2}$ cups puree.

3

5

3 Return the puree to a clean pan along with the sugar and heat gently, stirring, until the sugar has dissolved. Simmer until the required consistency is reached, stirring frequently to ensure even cooking and prevent sticking. A fruit butter is ready when it has the consistency of thick cream; a fruit cheese is ready when the spoon drawn across the base of the pan leaves a clear channel.

4 For a fruit butter, transfer to warm, sterilized jars or small pots (see page 11) and heat-process in a boiling-water canner. (See page 14).

5 For a fruit cheese, brush the inside of small, sterilized pots, molds, or straight-sided jars with vegetable oil and pour in the cheese; this will allow the cheese to be turned out once cool. Heat-process in a boiling-water canner. (See page 14).

NOTE It is not recommended to heat-process pumpkin or squash butters and cheeses in a boiling-water canner. Instead, they can be covered with secure-fitting lids and stored in the refrigerator for two to three weeks.

Candied, crystallized, and glacé fruits

Good candied, crystallized, and glacé fruits are expensive to buy, and the range of fruit that is available is limited. A wider range can be prepared at home without much difficulty. The process may seem rather long, but the results are worth it, and using a wire basket that fits inside the pan will make the process of lowering and removing the fruit from the pan simpler. Be sure to know the weight of the fruit prior to starting the recipe in order to determine how much sugar is to be used.

Making candied fruit

EQUIPMENT

For candied fruit:
Needle, cherry pitter, or
   sharp kitchen scissors
Kitchen scales (optional)
1 saucepan
Nonreactive bowl
Slotted spoon
Measuring cup
Wooden spoon
Tongs
Wire rack
Aluminum foil
Parchment paper

INGREDIENTS

Firm, ripe, undamaged
   fruit
Water
For each 1 lb prepared
   weight of fruit, 2¾ cups
   superfine sugar

1 Prepare the fruit: prick apricots, plums, and kumquats all over; remove the pits from cherries using a cherry pitter; peel citrus fruits (except kumquats) and divide into segments, removing all the pith and skin; peel, cut in half, and thickly slice pears, apples, and peaches; remove the "eyes" and the core of pineapples, and cut into rings or chunks.

2 Put the prepared fruit in one saucepan. Add just enough boiling water to cover, then simmer gently, covered, until tender; soft fruits take only two to three minutes, firm ones 10 to 15 minutes.

3 Using the slotted spoon, carefully transfer the fruit to a nonreactive bowl, leaving the cooking liquid in the pan.

4 Measure 1 ¼ cups of the cooking liquid for every 1 lb prepared weight of fruit into a saucepan. Add ¾ cup sugar and heat gently, stirring, until it has dissolved. Raise the heat and bring the syrup to the boil.

5 Pour the hot syrup over the fruit, cover, and leave in a cool place for one day. The next day, remove the fruit from the bowl, and pour the syrup back into the pan. Add another ¼ cup sugar to the syrup and heat gently, stirring, until it has dissolved. Bring to the boil, then remove from the heat and return the fruit to the pan. Cover and leave in a cool place for one day. Repeat this step for another five days so the syrup progressively becomes more concentrated.

3

4

5

Making candied fruit *continued*

6 After the fifth day, remove the fruit to a nonreactive bowl. Over a low heat, stir 6 tablespoons sugar into the remaining syrup until it has dissolved. Lower the fruit into the pan once more, and simmer gently for three to four minutes. Pour fruit and syrup into the nonreactive bowl, cover, and leave in a cool place for two days. Repeat this step once more, but instead of two days, leave the fruit for four days or up to two weeks.

7 Lift fruit from the syrup, using a pair of tongs, and carefully transfer each piece to a wire rack placed over a tray to dry. Cover with a dome of foil, making sure the foil does not touch the fruit, as protection against dust. Leave in a warm, dry place for two to three days, turning each piece over two or three times, until it is completely dry.

8 Using the tongs, pack the fruit into the containers, placing parchment paper between each layer.

Making crystallized fruit

1 Fill a small bowl with superfine sugar and bring a saucepan of water to a boil. Take each piece of dry candied fruit and dip it into the boiling water, using a skewer or tongs.

2 Allow any excess moisture to drain off, then roll the fruit in the sugar. Transfer to a foil-lined tray and leave to dry.

3 Using the tongs, pack the fruit into the containers, placing parchment paper between each layer.

Making glacé fruit

1 In the small saucepan, heat ⅔ cup water with the sugar and stir until it has dissolved. Boil for one minute, then pour a little of the hot syrup into the warmed cup or small bowl.

2 Cover the syrup in the pan. Place it over another pan filled with simmering water to keep warm.

3 Heat a pan of water until boiling. Using a skewer or tongs, dip each piece of fruit into the boiling water for 20 seconds, than dip into the cup of syrup. Transfer to a wire rack placed over a tray. As the syrup becomes cloudy, discard it and add fresh syrup.

4 Cover the rack with a dome of foil. Leave the fruit to dry in a warm place for two to three days, turning a few times.

5 Pack the fruit into containers, placing parchment paper between each layer.

Making canned fruit

Canning preserves by heat, which kills yeasts, molds, and microorganisms, and creates a vacuum to seal in the fruit. Only fruits (including tomatoes), which are acidic can safely be canned using this method; it is not possible to obtain the high temperatures needed to sterilize vegetables, meat, and fish unless using a pressure canner. The easiest and surest method to follow when canning whole fruit is to pack the fruit with a sugar syrup and process it in a boiling-water canner.

EQUIPMENT

Stainless steel knife
Cutting board
Saucepan (optional)
Heatproof measuring cup
Sterilized preserving
  jars and two-piece
  lids (see 11)
Boiling-water canner
Tongs
Wooden board
Labels

INGREDIENTS

Blemish-free, ripe fruit
Superfine or granulated
  sugar
Liquid: water or syrup
  (see step 3), and wine
  or a spirit (optional)
Flavorings, such as whole
  spices, citrus fruit peel,
  or liqueur (optional)

1 Prepare the fruit as the recipe specifies, and cook if necessary. Immerse pale fruits, such as pears and apples, in acidulated water (water with a small amount of vinegar, or lemon juice) if not being processed immediately. Rinse before packing. Prick gooseberry skins to prevent shrivelling. Soak rhubarb and strawberries in a sugar syrup for 12 hours.

2 Pack the fruit, cooked or raw, as closely as possible without crushing it, up to 1 inch from the tops of the sterilized jars. Fruits such as gooseberries and chopped rhubarb are best packed more tightly, but will need cooking before use. Apple slices may be "solid packed" so no liquid is added before or after processing; this prevents rising in the bottle.

Canning purees

Follow the basic steps, but pour the boiling, thick puree into hot, sterilized jars to within $1/2$ inch of the top, seal according to manufacturer's directions, and process in a boiling-water canner (see page 16). Then cool as normal.

Canning sauces and syrups

1 Put sterilized bottles in a low oven to warm. Prepare the sauce or syrup according to the recipe.

2 Pour the hot sauce or syrup through a funnel into the bottles to within 1 inch of the top. Seal the bottle according to the manufacturer's directions, and heat-process in a boiling-water canner (see page 16).

Bottling in alcohol

Alcohol can be used on its own (providing it is more than 40 percent proof) because nothing can grow in it. Or, to reduce the cost of the preserve, the alcohol can be combined with a sugar syrup.

1 Pack the fruit into sterilized jars, layering it with sugar.

2 Pour the alcohol into the jars to completely fill them, and swirl the jars to expel any air bubbles.

3 Seal the jars and store in a cool, dark, dry place for a least two months before eating, but preferably longer. Shake the jars every few days for the first month to help the sugar to dissolve.

Bottling in oil

Oil is not technically a preservative, but it protects ingredients immersed in it from contact with the air. Because of this, food immersed in oil must be treated beforehand by cooking, marinating in vinegar, drying, or salting (see pages 53). Oil preserves should not be kept as long as pickles or heat-processed foods, and should always be in the refrigerator.

3 Make a sugar syrup by gently heating the sugar and any flavorings being used in the water until the sugar is dissolved. Then, increase the heat and boil for 1 minute. To make a light syrup, use $1/2$ cup plus 1 tablespoon granulated sugar for every $2^1/2$ cups water. Pour the required hot liquid into prepared jars (see page 11), leaving about $1/2$ inch of headspace, and process in a boiling-water canner (see page 16).

Flavored vinegars, oils, and alcohols

Vinegar, oil, and alcohol are all excellent vehicles for infusing with flavoring ingredients; they inhibit the growth of microorganisms and they readily absorb flavors from other foods. Flavored vinegars, oils, and alcohols are very simple to make; usually, it is just a case of putting the flavorings in the bottle and pouring in the liquid to fill. They all share a number of common preparation points as well. Be sure to use very clean, sterilized equipment. Infuse with fresh herbs that have been washed, dried, and gently crushed to release the herbs' flavor oils. Always properly seal the jars that you are using. Finally, all need to be left for at least two to four weeks (shaken a few times) in a cool, dark, dry place before consuming. During the storage time, you can taste them to see if they have reached the degree of flavoring you want. When they are ready, strain out the flavoring ingredients. The exception is flavored alcohol, which matures over several months.

Flavored vinegars

These are usually based on white wine vinegar. Plain vinegars keep almost indefinitely, but it is better to use flavored vinegars within one year. A dash of flavored vinegar in a soup, casserole, or stew can really 'lift' its taste. It can also be used to add individuality to salad dressing and mayonnaise, or can be combined with other ingredients for marinades.

Rosemary and lime vinegar

$4\frac{1}{3}$ cups white wine vinegar
A few large sprigs of fresh rosemary
2 to 3 garlic cloves
1 lime, thinly sliced
MAKES $4\frac{1}{3}$ CUPS

Lemon and parsley vinegar

$4\frac{1}{3}$ cups white wine vinegar
2 to 3 garlic cloves
1 lime, thinly sliced
3 tablespoons chopped fresh parsley
Pared rind of 2 lemons
MAKES $4\frac{1}{3}$ CUPS

Hot chile vinegar

$4\frac{1}{3}$ cups white wine vinegar
$\frac{3}{4}$ lb mixed small red and green fresh chiles, sliced and seeded
2 to 3 garlic cloves
1 lime, thinly sliced
MAKES $4\frac{1}{3}$ CUPS

Orange vinegar

$4\frac{1}{3}$ cups white wine vinegar
Thinly pared zest, and juice, of 4 small oranges
1 tablespoon coriander seeds, lightly crushed (optional)
MAKES $4\frac{1}{3}$ CUPS

Raspberry Vinegar

1 lb raspberries
2 cups white wine vinegar
About $\frac{1}{2}$ cup granulated or superfine sugar, to taste

1 Put the raspberries in a nonreactive bowl. Add a little of the vinegar and mash the berries with a wooden spoon. Stir in the remaining vinegar. Cover and leave for two weeks, stirring occasionally.

2 Strain the vinegar through two layers of cheesecloth and pour into a nonreactive pan. Stir in the sugar and heat gently, stirring, until the sugar has dissolved. Simmer for 10 minutes. Leave to cool then bottle as normal.

MAKES ABOUT 2 CUPS

Spiced vinegar for pickling

1 tablespoon allspice berries
2 slim cinnamon sticks
1 tablespoon black peppercorns
1 tablespoon whole cloves
2 mace blades
2 bay leaves, torn in half
2 dried red chilies, seeded
5 cups white or red wine vinegar

Put all the ingredients into a nonreactive pan, bring to a boil, cool slightly, then pour into hot, sterilized bottles, distributing the spices evenly. Cover. The vinegar can be used after one day or, preferably, left in a cool, dark, dry place for one to two weeks. If it is kept for some time, strain out the flavorings before use.

MAKES 5 CUPS

Flavored oils

These are influenced by the quality and flavor of the base oil, so it is worth using a good quality, mild-flavored oil, such as canola, peanut, sunflower, safflower, or a mild olive oil. The taste of these oils will not dominate the infusing ingredients, unlike well-flavored oils, such as higher-quality olive and nut oils. Stay away from vegetable and corn oils, as they tend to have a heavy, coarse taste. Select small bottles, and store them in a cool, dark place because oils turn rancid fairly quickly, especially after opening. With proper storage, unopened bottles should keep for three to six months. Use flavored oil for making salad dressing, mayonnaise, and other oil-based sauces, or for dressing cooked vegetables, brushing on foods before grilling, roasting, or barbecuing, and even for frying, sautéing, and stir-frying. Even try drizzling it on good, crusty bread and eating it as is.

Herb and saffron oil

½ teaspoon saffron strands
2 fresh rosemary sprigs
2 fresh tarragon sprigs
2 bay leaves
4⅓ cups olive oil
⅔ cup walnut oil

Wrap the saffron in a small piece of kitchen foil and heat gently in a heavy skillet for about three minutes. Unwrap the saffron, put into a sterilized bottle, and add the remaining ingredients.

Continue as usual.

MAKES ABOUT 5 CUPS

Goat's milk cheese in oil

8 small, round patties of goat's milk cheese, such as chevre, weighing about 2½ oz each
2 bay leaves
3 fresh thyme sprigs
1 fresh rosemary sprig
6 black peppercorns
olive oil

Put the cheese, herbs, and peppercorns in a large, wide-necked jar. Carefully pour in the oil to cover completely. Cover the jar tightly and store in the refrigerator for two to three weeks before using. Use within six to eight weeks.

Flavored alcohol

This is usually made by layering the flavoring ingredient and sugar in a wide-necked bottle, pouring in the alcohol that is being used, such as brandy or gin, closing the bottles, and leaving in a dark place for at least three months, shaking occasionally for the first two weeks or so. The alcohols continue to improve for years. The flavorings can be left in the bottles or, once the drink is sufficiently infused, strained off through a nonreactive sieve.

Blackberry brandy

2 lb blackberries
Generous ½ cup sugar
750 ml bottle brandy

Lightly crush the blackberries with a wooden spoon before putting into a wide-necked bottle, and adding the brandy.

MAKES ABOUT 7 CUPS

Orange wine

Thinly pared zest of 2 large oranges
1¼ cups granulated or superfine sugar
4⅓ cups dry white wine
½ cup Armagnac or brandy

Bottle and seal as normal. Strain after two to three weeks. The wine is then ready for drinking.

MAKES 5 CUPS

Apricot cordial

About 1 cup dried apricots, coarsely chopped
2¼ cups dry white wine
Scant ½ cup clear honey
⅔ cup brandy

Macerate the apricots in the wine in a nonreactive bowl for 12 hours. Pour the contents of the bowl into a saucepan, bring slowly to a simmer, and stir in the honey until dissolved. Remove from the heat, cover, and leave in a cool place, but not the refrigerator, for three days, stirring occasionally. Strain, add the brandy, and bottle as normal. Store for two to three months before drinking.

MAKES 7 CUPS

Making pickles

Pickles are made from fruits and vegetables that have been preserved in vinegar; sometimes the vinegar is spiced or sweetened. Vegetables may be pickled raw or cooked. Most raw vegetables must be brined or salted before being pickled to draw out their moisture, which allows the vinegar to better penetrate the food. When vegetables and fruit are cooked, the cooking boils off excess moisture, and salt is not necessary.

EQUIPMENT

Sharp stainless steel knife
Cutting board
Weighted plate (optional)
Nonreactive bowl
   (optional)
Large, nonreactive pan
Piece of cheesecloth or
   gauze (optional)
Long piece of string
   (optional)
Long-handled wooden
   spoon
Paper towels or dishcloths
Sterilized jars (page 11)
Baking sheet or wooden
   board
Heatproof ladle or
   measuring cup
Nonreactive funnel
Clean dishcloth and hot,
   soapy water
Clean wide-necked jars,
   warmed
Parchment paper
Vinegar-proof lids

INGREDIENTS

Fruit or vegetables
Salt (optional)
Spices
Vinegar
Granulated or brown
   sugar (optional)

1 Prepare the vegetables or fruit as directed by the recipe. For raw vegetables either: layer them, sprinkling salt between each layer, then cover with a plate and leave overnight; or, completely cover and soak the vegetables in strong brine (see page 53). Put a weighted plate on the surface to ensure the vegetables are kept under the brine. Leave overnight.
For cooked fruits and vegetables that are to be pickled, prepare them according to the recipe. Drain very well and leave to dry.

2 Prepare the pickling vinegar according to the recipe. Let the vinegar cool; the spices can be left in or removed, depending on the strength of flavor required. For raw vegetables that were layered with salt, rinse off in cold running water, dry thoroughly with a clean cloth, and spread out on another clean, dry cloth and let air-dry completely. For raw vegetables that were soaked in brine, drain the brine, rinse the ingredients under cold running water, and dry thoroughly with a clean cloth to remove the rinsing water.

3 Put the sterilized jars on a baking sheet or wooden board.
Pack the vegetables into the sterilized jars to within 1 inch of the top. Be sure to pack them firmly so as not to leave too many air pockets, but not too tightly because the vinegar must be able to flow between them.

4 Depending on the type of pickle being made, whether a soft or crunchy result is desired or specified in the recipe, either use the pickling vinegar cold, or bring it to a boil. Pour or ladle into prepared jars (see page 11) to come to within $\frac{1}{2}$ inch of the top. Swirl the jars to expel any trapped air bubbles. If the pickles have a tendency to float to the tops of the jars, put a piece of crumpled parchment paper in the top of the jar. Remove it after a couple of weeks. Cover the jars with the vinegar-proof lids (see page 11). Store the pickles in a cool, dark, dry place for about two to three months before eating. The exception is red cabbage (see page 115).

Making soused fish

Oily fish that has been preserved, or pickled, in vinegar or another acid, such as lime juice, is commonly known by a number of different names, depending on the part of the world you are in. For example, in England we have soused mackerel and rollmop herrings; South Americans have seviche; and the Spanish have escabèche, where the fish is first cooked in oil and then steeped in vinegar or citrus juice.

EQUIPMENT

Sharp stainless steel knife
Cutting board
Large, nonreactive dish
Nonreactive measuring
  jug
Parchment paper

INGREDIENTS

Food to be pickled

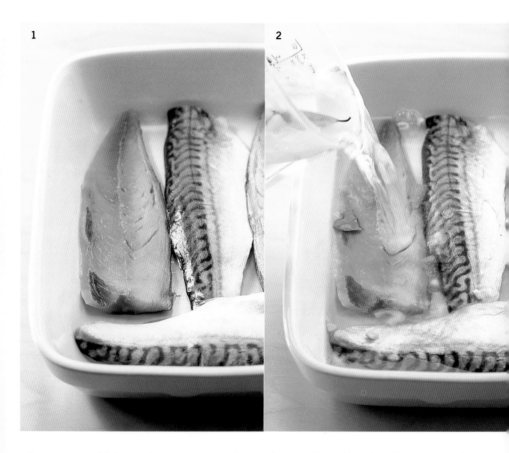

1 Prepare the fish by washing it, cutting off the fins, and discarding the heads. Put the fish, flat, in a large, nonreactive dish.

2 Pour the pickling liquid, made according to the recipe, over the fish.

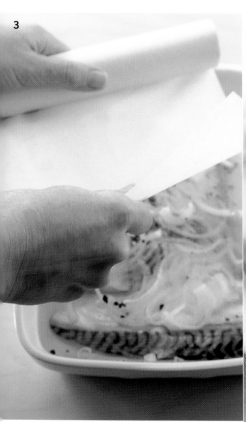

3 Cover the dish with a double thickness of parchment paper and bake at 300°F until the fish is very soft, 1 ¼ to 1 ½ hours for mackerel fillets.

4 Leave the fish to cool in the liquid. Keep, covered, in the refrigerator for two to three days.

Making chutney

Chutneys are mixtures of chopped vegetables and fruit cooked together with vinegar, sugar, and spices. The chutney is simmered slowly until the ingredients have softened and nearly all the liquid has evaporated. A test for doneness is drawing a spoon drawn across the bottom of a pan; if the channel left by the spoon does not immediately fill with liquid, the chutney is ready. Chutneys vary in their fruitiness, spiciness, and sweet-and-sour combination.

EQUIPMENT

Sharp stainless steel knife

Cutting board

Small piece of cheesecloth, or spice bag (optional)

Long piece of string (optional)

Long-handled wooden spoon

Baking sheet or wooden board

Heatproof ladle or measuring cup

Nonreactive funnel

Clean dishcloth and hot soapy water

Sterilized jars, warmed (see page 11)

Boiling-water canner

Labels

INGREDIENTS

Vegetables

Fruit (fresh or dried)

Vinegar

Spices

Sugar

1 Prepare the vegetables and fruit; cut into small pieces and put in the pan with the vinegar and spices. If a spice bag is being used, put the spices in a small piece of cheesecloth and tie with string, and then tie the loose end of the string to the handle of the pan to suspend the bag in the contents. Bring to a boil and simmer, uncovered, until the vegetables and fruit are soft but not mushy, anything between 30 minutes and 1 ½ hours. Stir occasionally to prevent sticking.

2 Over low heat, stir in the sugar until it has dissolved, then return to a boil and cook until the mixture is thick. Stir as necessary to prevent sticking. Lift up the spice bag, press it against the side of the pan to extract the juices, then discard the bag. The chutney is ready when it is thick and no liquid appears in the channel that is left when the spoon is drawn across the bottom of the pan. It will thicken further upon standing.

3 Prepare the jars (see page 11) and
fill. Heat-process in a boiling-water
canner. (See page 14).

Preserving with fat

Food such as meat, poultry, game, and fish can be preserved by pouring a layer of melted fat over the surface, which sets and forms a hermetic seal and thereby excludes air from contact with the food. Examples are potted meats, such as rillettes, confits, and pâtés. All equipment you use must be scrupulously clean to ensure that the food will not spoil. Stored in a cold place, these foods should last up to three to four weeks, depending on the recipe. Once the fat covering is broken, the food must be eaten within a day or so.

Potting

EQUIPMENT

Cooking pot, such as a casserole

Forks, food processor, or blender, according to the recipe

Sterilized small containers, such as earthenware ramekins, individual soufflé dishes, or pots

INGREDIENTS

Ingredients according to the recipe

Fat, either from the recipe or additional

Meat, poultry, game, and fish are cooked, usually fried or baked, before being tightly packed into pots and sealed with fat.

1 Cook the food slowly and thoroughly according to the recipe. This draws out the moisture and fat.

2 Pour off the liquid and fat; reserve the fat.

3 Puree or shred the food, according to the recipe.

4 Pack the food into the containers making sure there are no air pockets. Smooth the surface and refrigerate for three to four hours until completely cold.

5 Gently heat the reserved fat, then pour over the food to form a layer at least $^1\!/_2$-inch thick over the entire surface. Leave undisturbed in a cold place until set.

6 Cover the container and keep in the refrigerator for up to three to four weeks, depending on the recipe.

Making pâté

The meat, poultry, game, or fish is cooked in the container. Commercially produced pâtés sometimes contain preservatives to extend their shelf life.

1 Prepare the ingredients according to the recipe.

2 Line the terrine with some of the caul fat, pork back fat, or bacon.

3 Pack the prepared ingredients into the terrine, pushing them well into the corners to make sure there are no air pockets. Tap the container on the work surface to release any air that may have become trapped.

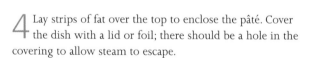

4 Lay strips of fat over the top to enclose the pâté. Cover the dish with a lid or foil; there should be a hole in the covering to allow steam to escape.

5 Put the terrine in a roasting pan, place it on the oven rack, and pour in enough water to come halfway up the sides of the dish. Bake according to the recipe until the pâté has shrunk from the sides of the dish and the fat is oozing around the sides. Remove from the roasting pan and let cool.

6 Cover the cool but not cold pâté with parchment paper. Place weights on the top and leave until cold. Refrigerate for at least one day; eat within three days.

Drying

Traditionally the drying effect of the sun or the wind has been utilized to extend the storage of a wide range of foods – fruit, vegetables, beans, meats, sausages, and fish. Today, drying is mainly done commercially with special equipment. At home, the choice is limited to specific fruits, vegetables, and herbs as well as some aromatics such as orange peel. Drying meats, such as sausage, and fish requires special, precise conditions to be successful and safe. Sun and outdoor drying give the best flavor to foods, but most of us do not live in suitable climates with steadily warm, dry temperatures and plenty of ventilation and clean air. Instead, we have to use either the oven or indoor air-drying.

Oven-drying

The food will not always match the appearance of most commercial products where specific varieties are chosen and are treated to make sure they retain their color.

EQUIPMENT

Sharp stainless steel knife
Cutting board
Wire rack
Aluminum foil
Parchment paper

INGREDIENTS

Foods to be dried

1 Select good quality, firm ingredients that are free of blemishes. Fruit should be just ripe, and peeled if necessary with cores or pits removed. Root and tuber vegetables usually dry better than leaves or stalks.

2 Thinly slice and blanch vegetables, except tomatoes, sweet peppers, okra, mushrooms, beets and onions. Remove or trim mushrooms stalks. Halve tomatoes, and halve and pit peaches and plums.

3 Dip foods that discolor, such as apples and pears, in a solution of 6 tablespoons lemon juice to $4\frac{1}{3}$ cups water.

Oven-drying times

Apple rings	6 to 8 hours
Apricots, halved and pitted	36 to 48 hours
Bananas, peeled and halved lengthwise	10 to 16 hours
Berries, left whole	12 to 18 hours
Cherries, pitted	18 to 24 hours
Herbs, tied in bundles	12 to 16 hours
Peaches, peeled, halved, and pitted	36 to 48 hours
sliced	12 to 16 hours
Pears, peeled, halved, and cored	36 to 48 hours
Pineapple, cored and cut into ¼-inch rings	36 to 48 hours
Plums, halved	18 to 24 hours
Vegetables, ¼-inch slices	2 hours
Vegetables, ½-inch slices	7 to 8 hours

4 Put a wire rack on a foil-lined baking sheet. Arrange the food on the rack leaving space between the pieces. Halved fruit should be set cut-side down. Set the oven to its lowest setting (it should not exceed 140°F); the warming oven of a cast-iron cooker is ideal. Put the rack of food in the oven and prop the door slightly open (not applicable for a cast-iron cooker).

5 Half way through drying, turn the food over. If using more than one shelf at a time, swap the trays from one shelf to the other. Leave the food until it is dry and leathery.

6 Leave to cool before packing in layers between sheets of parchment paper in airtight containers. Store in a cool place but not the refrigerator.

Air-drying

1 Prepare the fruit or vegetables, and treat for discoloration, if necessary (see left).

2 Spread on racks on baking sheets; using thick thread, thread onto lengths of thin sticks, keep the food slightly separated to allow air to circulate around the pieces. Place across a roasting or baking pan.

3 Leave in a warm and dry place (not a steamy kitchen), for example, in a warm cupboard, or above a central heating boiler. The food is ready when it is dried and shriveled.

Air-drying herbs

Herbs with firm leaves, such as thyme and rosemary, can be dried more successfully than soft, fleshy herbs like basil.

1 Choose herbs shortly before they come into flower. Pick them in the morning as soon as the dew has lifted but before the sun has become too hot. If drying the herbs in bunches, pick stems as long as possible.

2 To dry in bunches, tie the herbs loosely in small bundles with thick thread and suspend in a warm, dry place out of direct sunlight. They should be ready in three days.

3 Alternatively, spread the herbs on a wire rack covered with cheesecloth (which allows the air to circulate) and leave in a warm cupboard for three to five days.

4 Herbs can also be dried tied in paper bags with small holes cut in the bags, and left in a warm, dry place for three days.

5 Herbs are ready when the stems and leaves are brittle but retain their green color, and crumble easily when rubbed between the fingers. Either keep the stems and leaves intact, or strip the leaves off, and store in an airtight container in a cool, dark, dry place.

Using a dehydrator

If planning to dry large quantities, it may be worthwhile to buy a domestic dehydrator. They are relatively expensive to purchase, but are economical to run, as well as being efficient, flexible, and easy to use. Consult the manufacturer's manual for precise instructions.

1 Arrange the prepared food, spaced slightly apart, on the stackable trays.

2 Set the thermostat. Insert the trays in the dehydrator and put on the lid. Leave for the specified length of time; there is no need to rotate the trays.

3 Remove the trays from the dehydrator and leave the food to cool completely before being packed and stored.

Curing

Curing is a method of preserving food by impregnating it with salt or a salt solution, called brine, which draws out the moisture from the food, so inhibiting the growth of bacteria. Nowadays, foods are not as heavily salted as they used to be, and as a result, do not keep as long. Meticulous hygiene and a temperature of no more than 40°F in an airy, insect-free environment are vital. As saltpetre is very difficult to obtain domestically, home-cured foods must be treated as fresh foods.

Brining

EQUIPMENT

Nonreactive saucepan

Nonreactive slotted
  spoon

Nonreactive sieve

Nonreactive measuring
  cup

Deep earthenware crock,
  or similar nonreactive
  container that will hold
  the food

Plate to just fit inside the
  top of the dish

Nonreactive weights

INGREDIENTS

Sea salt

Sugar (optional,
  according to the recipe)

Flavorings, such as herbs
  and spices, according
  to the recipe

Food to be cured

To preserve meat without saltpeter, the brine strength needs to be 10 percent, but a less concentrated solution is used at home to produce simple salted meats for immediate cooking. The meat will lack the customary pink color of store-bought cured meats. The length of time the meat is kept in the brine depends not only on the size and shape of the food, but also how salty you want it to be.

1 Make a brine solution by stirring 6 cups salt into $12\frac{1}{2}$ cups water using a wooden spoon, in a non-corrosive container. Add $1\frac{1}{3}$ cups soft brown sugar and flavorings according to the recipe, for example, 2 tablespoons juniper berries, crushed, 3 bay leaves, several sprigs of thyme. Skim the surface with the slotted spoon, leave until cold, then strain with the sieve.

2 Put the food to be brined in the dish. Pour the cold brine over the food, making sure it is completely covered. Cover with a plate. If necessary, weight the plate to ensure the food stays under the liquid.

3 Leave in a cool, dry, well-ventilated, insect-free place, or the refrigerator, for the specified time, about 7 to 10 days for a small leg of pork. Check daily to make sure the brine is still "sweet," with no off odors or a "ropey" consistency, although it might be slimy.

4 Remove the food from the brine and rinse well. The food can now be cooked.

Dry salting

EQUIPMENT

Deep earthenware crock, or similar nonreactive container that will hold the food

Wooden spoon

INGREDIENTS

Food to be cured

Salt

Flavorings, such as herbs and spices, according to the recipe

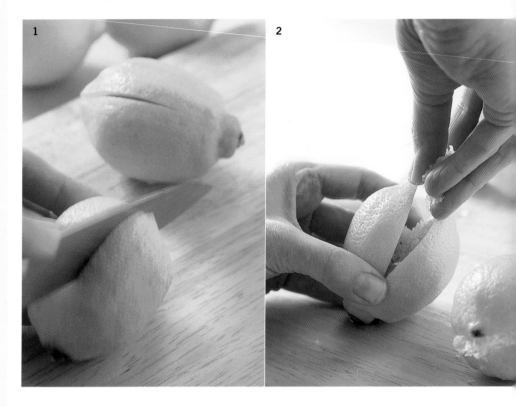

1 Prepare the food as indicated in the recipe.

2 Mix the salt and any flavorings. Sprinkle a thick layer of salt over the base of the dish.

3 Lay the food on the salt and spoon salt between it and the sides of the dish. Cover the food with a thick layer of salt.

4 Leave in a cool, dry place or the refrigerator, for the specified time, according to the size and thickness of the food and the degree of salting required. Some recipes specify rubbing salt into the food.

5 To serve, drain off the liquid that comes from the food.

NOTE If salting meat, rinse off all the salt and hang the food in a cold, dry, well-ventilated, insect-free place to dry before storing in the refrigerator. To cook the meat straight away, soak it in cold water overnight then drain. Put into a large pan, cover with cold water and add a bouquet garni, parsley sprigs, quartered onions, chopped carrots and some juniper berries. Bring to a boil then simmer very gently for 25 to 30 minutes per pound, topping up the water if necessary. Serve hot or cold (leave it to cool in the liquid, in a cold place).

How to cure ham

"Ham" is not a single product that is always produced in the same way – Italian prosciutto is quite different from robust Black Forest ham. All ham is made from the hind legs of pigs that are bred for the purpose, and most ham is cured in salt, but beyond that, the flavor depends on many different factors, including the breed, age, and diet of the pig. It also depends on the type of salt-curing (whether in brine or dry-packed), the length of curing and aging, whether the ham is smoked or air-dried, what type of wood is used for the smoking, and even the actual air in which the ham is dried.

The two most commonly used methods of salt-curing ham are sweet-pickle curing, in which the meat is submerged in a vat of brine, and injection-curing, in which the ham is injected with brine. Sometimes, the two processes are combined to speed up the curing process. Dry curing, which involves the repeated rubbing of salt over the surface of the meat, is a slow, labor-intensive process, and therefore expensive, but it ensures the use of minimum salt for preservation and gives a better quality product. In either case, extra preservatives are often added to the cure, in the form of saltpeter (potassium nitrate), which also gives ham its pink color, herbs, spices, and other flavorings such as wine. Honey, brown sugar, or molasses may also be used.

Once the ham has been given the required degree of salt curing, surplus salt is removed. At this point, the ham can be sold as is, partially smoked, fully smoked, air-dried, or a combination of smoked and air-dried. The time and method that is chosen varies from place to place: in some, the ham is smoked by being buried in wood ash; elsewhere, it is hung in a cool, dry, airy place, without being smoked, to air-dry; in other places, it is smoked over fragrant wood-like oak, hickory, and fruit woods.

There are two main types of ham, raw hams, such as prosciutto, Bayonne ham, and Westphalian ham, and cooked hams, such as York ham and Smithfield ham, which are boiled in stock or baked before eating.

Smoking

Smoking helps to inhibit the growth of microorganisms, as well as imparts a characteristic flavor into the food. It was originally combined with salting or drying as a means of preserving food, but today smoking is used more for flavoring than preservation. There are two methods of smoking – hot and cold.

Hot-smoking

EQUIPMENT
Nonreactive container
Hot smoker
Fuel

INGREDIENTS
Salt
Food to be smoked, e.g. whole fish or fillets, piece of meat or chicken, sausages

Hot smoking can be done at home in a number of ways. For example, it can be done Chinese-style in a covered wok or deep pan, or using a special type of barbecue or kettle smoker, or using a purpose-built home smoker, some of which are small enough to be used indoors if the ventilation is adequate. In hot-smoking, the temperature is raised to between 180°F and 212°F depending on the food, which serves to cook the food, but does not preserve it. Therefore, it must be refrigerated and eaten within a day or so.

1 If you like, sprinkle a thick layer of salt over the food, lay it in a nonreactive container, cover, and leave in a cold place, about three to four hours, depending on the food. Rinse under cold running water to remove excess salt, and dry thoroughly. Alternatively, the food can be marinated.

2 Put the food, spaced apart, on the rack of the smoker, or suspend it on a hook from the lid.

3 Sprinkle the wood shavings, such as oak, beech, or fruit wood on the bottom of the smoker; flavorings such as whole spices or herbs can also be added. Put the trivet, containing water or other liquid, on top. Either put the rack with the food on it in place, or put on the lid.

How cold-smoked salmon is made

Producing traditional smoked salmon that is consistently good is not an easy task. The first requirement is high quality salmon. Then, it takes expertise to be able to adjust the time the fish is in contact with the salt, the drying time, and the smoking time to suit the particular size, texture, and fattiness of the fish. The correct temperature throughout the smoking process must also be maintained according to the particulars of the salmon one is using. Local methods for preparing smoked salmon, the "secrets" of each individual smoker, and the type of flavor one is hoping to achieve also influences the way in which salmon is smoked. For example, Scottish salmon is usually given a milder cure than salmon intended for lox.

After arrival at the smokery, the salmon is thoroughly cleaned and filleted. Then, it can either be dry-salted or soaked in brine to draw out the natural juices, which, if left in, would make the fish too moist and would cause it to stew rather than cook through smoking in the oven. This takes anywhere from a few hours to twelve, or even as many as twenty-four. Next, the salt or brine is washed off and the fillets are hung in the cold smokehouse for a few hours to "drip dry" before being smoked.

Depending on the style of the smoker, the fish may be wiped with a cloth soaked in whisky and/or rubbed with sugar, usually brown sugar. If smoked salmon is dark red or deep orange, dye will also have been added.

The precise fuel for smoking varies from one smokehouse to another. Traditional smokers use wood shavings from old whisky or sherry casks made from oak, and sold by old-style cooperages. In Britain, oak chips or shavings are the usual fuel, while hickory is favored in the United States. Juniper, beech, even heather may also be used. The shavings or chips are soaked in water before being lit, so they smoulder rather than burn during the smoking process.

The fish may be laid on shelves or suspended on hooks. The doors are shut and the salmon is left for the required time and temperature. For cold-smoked salmon, it is usually between seven and eight hours at around 75°F, after which the fish will be succulent and smokey.

The salmon is left to cool completely. It may then be left whole, or cut into wafer thin slices and vacuum-packed.

4 Light the fuel that supplies the heat, and ignite the wood shavings that create the smoke. Leave for the specified time in the recipe instructions, if available. For example, a trout takes about 35 to 45 minutes, depending on the temperature, size, and degree of smoky flavor required. Apply the normal tests for when cooking is complete; fish should flake easily and chicken juices should run clear.

5 Remove the food from the smoker and either eat immediately, or let cool completely, cover, and keep in the refrigerator for up to two days.

Freezing

Freezing at a temperature below 0°F preserves food by immobilizing the bacteria that can spoil food, and slows down the enzyme activity that can cause quality deterioration. Food should be frozen quickly to prevent the formation of large ice crystals that damage cell walls, so that the thawed food doesn't lose its liquid and "collapse." Conversely, thawing should be done slowly.

EQUIPMENT

Freezer-proof containers; polythene bags, plastic wrap, aluminum foil, plastic boxes.

Foods that do not freeze successfully

Whole strawberries

Whole tomatoes

Garlic

Eggs in the shell

Hard-boiled eggs

Creams with a fat content below 40 per cent

Emulsion sauces such as mayonnaise

Recipes with sauces thickened with eggs

Potatoes

Cooked joints of meat

1 If freezing more than 2 lb of food, turn the freezer thermostat to "fast-freeze." Choose heavyweight, vapor- and moisture-proof containers and wrappings to protect the food from freezer burn. For example, thick polythene bags, plastic wrap, foil, and plastic boxes.

2 Prepare the food as necessary and make sure that it is completely cold.

3 Vegetables should be blanched to preserve their color, flavor, texture, and nutritional content, and to destroy the enzymes which would otherwise cause deterioration during frozen storage. Put the prepared vegetables, in batches if necessary so the pan is not crowded, in a wire basket. Plunge into a large saucepan of boiling water, cover and return quickly to the boil. Boil for the specified time. Remove the basket and immediately plunge it into a large bowl of water with some ice cubes in it. When cold, drain the vegetables very well.

4 Blackberries, black and red currants, blueberries, gooseberries, and raspberries can be "open-frozen" by spreading them on trays lined with parchment paper (see above) and freezing before packing as normal.

5 Frosted and decorated cakes can also be open-frozen until firm before wrapping closely.

6 Pack the food into suitable containers. If solid food is in a rigid container that it does not fill, fill the gap with crumpled tissue paper (wait until decorated cakes are frozen). Leave 1-inch headspace in rigid containers of liquids to allow for expansion, then fill the space if necessary.

7 Sauces, soups, purees, casseroles, etc. can be poured into polythene bags set in freezer-proof rectangular or square containers, 1-inch headspace to allow for expansion (see left). Freeze until solid, then remove the bag from the container, seal and label.

8 When the food is frozen, return the thermostat to the normal setting.

9 With a few exceptions, such as vegetables and fish that can be cooked from a frozen state, food should be thawed in the refrigerator before using.

10 To freeze herbs, open freeze parsley sprigs, then pack into freezer-proof polythene bags without crushing the herbs, and tie the bags fairly loosely. Chopped herbs can be frozen individually or combined into blends, such as Provençal – with basil, oregano, thyme, parsley and rosemary – and then either packed into small freezer bags or small containers and put inside a labelled freezer box. Or, put the herbs (preferably in useful quantities, such as 2 tablespoonfuls) into ice cube trays, cover with water and freeze. The frozen cubes can be put into freezer bags or boxes. Use frozen herbs straight from the freezer without thawing.

Storage times

MEAT, UNCOOKED	
Beef	8 months
Lamb	6 months
Pork	6 months
Freshly minced meat	3 months
Liver	3 months
Sausages	3 months
Ham and other smoked meats	1 to 2 months
Bacon, smoked	2 months
Bacon, unsmoked	1 month
Bacon slices, smoked	2 months
Bacon slices, unsmoked	1 month
MEAT, COOKED	
Casseroles, stews, etc.	2 months
POULTRY AND GAME, UNCOOKED	
Chicken	12 months
Turkey	6 months
Duck and game birds	6 months
Venison	12 months
FISH, UNCOOKED	
White or oily fish	3 months
Smoked fish	6 weeks
Shellfish	1 month
DAIRY PRODUCE	
Butter, unsalted	6 months
Butter, salted	3 months
Cream, above 40% fat	3 months
Soft cheeses	6 weeks
Hard cheeses	3 months
Hard cheeses, grated	6 months
Milk	1 month
BAKED GOODS	
Bread and rolls, crisp	1 month
Bread, white and brown	6 months
Cakes, uncooked	1 month
Cakes, cooked and undecorated	4 months
Pastry, unbaked	3 months
Pastry, baked	6 months
VEGETABLES	
Most vegetables	12 months
Mushrooms, raw	1 month
Mushrooms, cooked	3 months
Onions	3 months
Herbs	6 months

2 Perfect preserves

Honey-spiced apple jelly

Tart cooking apples, coarsely
  chopped, without coring or
  peeling (see method)
Water (see method)
Sugar (see method)
Honey (see method)
Whole cloves (see method)
Piece of fresh ginger (see method)
Cinnamon sticks (see method)

EACH 2$\frac{1}{2}$ CUPS JUICE MAKES
3 CUPS JELLY

This was one of my country grandmother's recipes, made with the "fallers"
we used to collect from beneath old apple trees in the orchard. The
combination of warm spices, honey, and apple makes for a very special jelly,
with a softer texture than jellies sweetened entirely with sugar.

1 Put the apples in a pan with
2$\frac{1}{2}$ cups water for every 2 pounds
of apples. Simmer gently, uncovered,
until the fruit is very soft.

2 Pour the contents of the pan into a
jelly bag suspended over a nonreactive
bowl and leave overnight in a cool
place to drip.

3 Discard the pulp in the jelly bag.
Measure the juice into a clean pan.
For each 2$\frac{1}{2}$ cups of juice, add a scant
2 cups sugar, $\frac{1}{3}$ cup honey, and a
cheesecloth bag filled with 3 whole

cloves, a small piece of fresh ginger,
and a 2-inch long cinnamon stick.
Heat gently to dissolve the sugar and
honey, then bring to the boil and boil
rapidly until the setting point is
reached (see page 23).

4 Discard the spice bag. Prepare and
fill the jars (see page 11), then heat-
process in a boiling-water canner
(see page 14). Leave to cool. Label
the jars and store in a cool, dark, dry
place for two to three days before
eating. Use within one year.

Apple and fig chutney

3 lb tart cooking apples, cored and
  chopped
3 lb onion, chopped
2$\frac{3}{4}$ cups dried figs, chopped
2$\frac{1}{2}$ cups white wine vinegar
4 teaspoons ground ginger
$\frac{1}{2}$ teaspoon cayenne pepper
$\frac{2}{3}$ cup dark brown sugar

MAKES ABOUT 12 CUPS

This dark, sweet, spicy chutney goes very well with sharp, mature
Cheddar cheese and smoked chicken.

1 Put all the ingredients except the
brown sugar into a nonreactive pan
and bring to a boil over a medium
heat.

2 Reduce the heat to low and
simmer gently, uncovered, until
the apples are tender.

3 Keeping the mixture over low heat,
stir in the sugar. When it has
dissolved, simmer gently, uncovered,
for about 1$\frac{1}{2}$ hours, stirring as
necessary to prevent sticking. The

chutney is ready when no liquid
appears in the channel that is left
when the spoon is drawn across
the bottom of the pan. It will
thicken further upon standing.

4 Prepare the jars and fill (see page
11), then heat-process in a boiling-
water canner (see page 14). Leave
until cool before labeling and storing
in a cool, dark, dry place for at least
six weeks before eating. Use within
one year.

Opposite: Honey-spiced apple jelly

Bottled apricots with vanilla

Apricot and orange butter

Orange rind and juice enhance the flavor of the apricots in this recipe.
For a special treat and an even more pronounced apricot flavor, add two
to four tablespoons apricot liqueur just before the end of the cooking.

3 lb ripe apricots, halved and pitted
2 oranges, zested and juiced
Water (see method)
Sugar (see method)

MAKES 6 CUPS

1 Put the apricots, orange rind, and orange juice in a nonreactive pan and add enough water to just cover. Simmer gently, uncovered, for about 45 minutes, stirring occasionally with a wooden spoon, until the fruit is very soft. Remove from the heat.

2 Using a wooden spoon, press the apricot pulp through a fine sieve into a clean pan. For each 2 1/2 cups puree, add 1 3/4 cups sugar and heat gently, stirring, until the sugar has dissolved. Bring to a boil over a high heat and boil rapidly for 30 to 40 minutes, stirring frequently, until the mixture is thick. Remove from the heat.

3 Prepare and fill the jars (see page 11), then heat-process in a boiling-water canner (see page 14). Leave to cool. Label the jars and store in a cool, dark, dry place for one week before eating. Use within one year.

Bottled apricots with vanilla

Instead of using whole vanilla beans, strips of orange rind or cinnamon
sticks can be added to the jars for a different flavor. Or, you could
experiment with more exotic spices such as cardamom and star anise.

About 3 lb firm but
** ripe apricots**
2/3 cup sugar
1/2 cup freshly squeezed lemon juice
2 1/2 cups water
2 whole vanilla beans

MAKES ABOUT 10 CUPS

1 Immerse the apricots in a pan of gently boiling water for 20 to 30 seconds. Immediately remove the apricots from the water and peel off their skins using a small sharp knife or your fingers, if they come off easily. Leave to cool.

2 Put the sugar, lemon juice, and water in a saucepan over a low heat, stirring, until the sugar has dissolved. Bring to a boil.

3 Add the apricots to the syrup, in batches if necessary, and poach for 10 minutes.

4 Using a slotted spoon, immediately transfer the apricots to two warm, sterilized 5-cup jars. Slit the vanilla beans lengthwise with a knife and add two halves to each jar.

5 When all the apricots have been removed from the pan, boil the syrup for five minutes. Pour into prepared jars (see page 11) to within 1/2 inch of the top. Swirl the jars to expel any air bubbles and seal them. Process in a boiling-water canner (see page 16).

6 Store in a cool, dark, dry place for one month before eating. Use within 12 to 18 months.

Apricot tart

1 ⅓ cups flour
½ teaspoon baking powder
Pinch of salt
¼ cup superfine sugar
1 ¼ sticks chilled butter, diced
1 egg yolk
Few drops of vanilla extract
2 tablespoons water
1 ¼ cups heavy cream (whisked to
   form soft peaks)
1 cup mascarpone cheese
7 Bottled Apricots with Vanilla, well-
   drained and halved (see page 65)
4 tablespoons liquid from the Bottled
   Apricots with Vanilla
3 tablespoons strained apricot jam
3 tablespoons almond liqueur

SERVES 6

To make a lighter, but equally quick filling for
this tart, substitute ricotta cheese or strained
yogurt that has been beaten until smooth, for
the mascarpone cheese.

1 Stir the flour, baking powder, salt, and sugar
together in a bowl. Cut in the butter with a pastry
blender or two knives until the mixture resembles
crumbs. Add the egg yolk, vanilla extract, and water
and mix to form a dough; if it is too dry, add a little
more water. Turn out on to a lightly floured surface
and knead briefly until smooth. Cover and chill
for 30 minutes.

2 Using a 9-inch tart pan with a removable
bottom, roll out the pastry until it is 2 inches
larger than the diameter of the pan. Prick the
base and freeze for 1 hour.

3 Preheat the oven to 400°F. Line the pastry-
covered tart pan with parchment paper and pie
weights. Bake for 15 minutes, then remove the pie
weights and bake for another 8 to 10 minutes until
golden. Transfer the tart pan to a wire rack to cool.

4 Beat the mascarpone cheese with a wooden
spoon or hand-held whisk and fold into the heavy
cream. Spread evenly on the cooled tart pan.

5 Arrange the apricot halves on the filling. Boil
the liquid from the apricot jar with the jam and
liqueur until syrupy then brush over the apricots.
Chill for 15 minutes.

Blackberry fruit cheese

Blackberry and apple jam with cardamom

Blackberry and apple go together so well they seem to be one of "nature's partnerships." In this recipe, a slightly spicy note has been added by the inclusion of a few cardamom seeds, which highlight the taste of the fruit.

¾ lb tart cooking apples, peeled, cored, and cut into chunks
⅔ cup water
2 lb blackberries
Scant 3 cups sugar
Seeds from 3 cardamom pods, lightly crushed
Half a lemon, juiced

MAKES ABOUT 6 CUPS

1 Put the apples and water in a preserving pan, bring to a boil over a high heat, then reduce heat and simmer very gently for about 15 minutes until the apples are soft.

2 Add the blackberries and sugar to the pan and cook gently for a few minutes until they are soft and the juices begin to run. Tie the cardamom seeds in a cheesecloth bag and add to the pan with the lemon juice.

Bring to a boil and cook for 15 minutes or until the setting point is reached (see page 23).

3 Scoop out and discard the spice bag. Prepare the jars and fill (see page 11), then heat-process in a boiling-water canner (see page 14). Leave to cool. Label the jars and store in a cool, dark, dry place for at least three weeks before eating. Use within one year.

Blackberry fruit cheese

This is another of my country grandmother's recipes for using the produce from her orchard, coupled with blackberries from the New Forest in Hampshire, England, where she lived.

2¼ lb blackberries
1 lb tart cooking apples, chopped
2½ cups water
Sugar (see method)

MAKES ABOUT 4 CUPS

1 Put the blackberries, apples, and water into a nonreactive pan and cook over a low heat for about 30 minutes until the fruit is very soft. Remove from the heat.

2 Using a wooden spoon, press the pulp through a fine sieve into a clean pan. For each 2¼ cups puree, add 2¼ cups sugar and heat gently, stirring, until the sugar has dissolved. Then, bring to a boil, reduce the

heat, and simmer for 40 to 60 minutes, stirring frequently, until the mixture is very thick.

3 Remove the pan from the heat. Prepare the jars and fill (see page 11), then heat-process in a boiling-water canner (see page 14). Leave to cool. Label the molds and store in a cool, dark, dry place for one week before eating. Use within one year.

Grapefruit and honey marmalade

2 large grapefruit, about 2 lb in total
4 lemons
7½ cups water
5 cups sugar
¾ cup honey

MAKES 9 CUPS

The honey gives a delicate set to this lovely marmalade, which goes particularly well with croissants.

1 Peel the grapefruit as you would an orange, then cut the pith from the peel; reserve the pith. Using a vegetable peeler, peel the rinds from the lemons as thinly as possible and remove the pith from the fruit, reserving it. Shred all the peel finely.

2 Coarsely chop the grapefruit and lemon flesh, reserving any seeds and saving the juice. Tie the seeds and pith in a cheesecloth bag with a long length of string. Put the flesh, peel, reserved juice, and water in a nonreactive pan. Tie the cheesecloth bag to the handle of the pan so it is suspended in the contents.

3 Bring to a boil, then simmer for about 1½ hours until the peel is tender and the contents of the pan are reduced by half. Remove the cheesecloth bag and squeeze it firmly against the side of the pan to extract the liquid.

4 Over low heat, stir in the sugar and honey until the sugar has dissolved, then bring to a boil over a high heat and boil hard for 15 to 20 minutes until the setting point is reached (see page 23).

5 Remove any scum with a slotted spoon, and let the marmalade stand off the heat for 15 minutes. Stir to distribute the peel. Prepare the jars and fill (see page 11), then heat-process in a boiling-water canner (see page 14). Let cool overnight, label the jars, and store in a cool, dark, dry place for up to one year.

Pink grapefruit curd

Peeled pink grapefruit segments are added to the curd halfway through the cooking to give the finished product an interesting appearance, texture and flavor. For the best color, use ruby red grapefruit rather than ordinary pink grapefruit.

1 Put the grapefruit zest and juice, lemon zest and juice, and butter in a heatproof bowl set over a pan of gently simmering water. Cook, stirring frequently, until the butter has melted.

2 Stir in the sugar and eggs and continue to cook for 25 to 40 minutes, stirring frequently at first, then constantly until the mixture is thick enough to coat the back of the spoon; a slightly thinner mixture will thicken in the refrigerator (although

it will remain a soft curd). Add the grapefruit segments after about 15 to 30 minutes. Do not allow the water in the pan to boil or the mixture will curdle.

3 Prepare the jars and fill (see page 11), then seal and leave to cool (see page 29). Label and store in the refrigerator for up to three months, unopened. Eat within three to four days of opening.

1 pink or ruby red grapefruit, zested and juiced
2 lemons, zested and juiced
$\frac{3}{4}$ cup unsalted butter, diced
2 cups superfine sugar
5 large eggs, beaten and strained
1 pink or ruby red grapefruit, divided into segments, without skin or pith

MAKES ABOUT 3½ CUPS

Steamed pink grapefruit curd pudding

A generous amount of the grapefruit curd is spooned into the mold before the pudding mixture is added, so the grapefruit flavor slightly permeates the cooked pudding, flowing down its sides and surrounding it in a lake of luscious sauce.

1 Spoon the pink grapefruit curd into a heatproof pudding mold; set aside. Put a trivet in the bottom of a large saucepan. Pour enough water into the pan to come halfway up the sides of the mold. Cover the pan and bring to the boil.

2 Beat the butter with the sugar with a wooden spoon until light and fluffy, then gradually beat in the eggs. Add the lemon zest and juice. Sift the flour and baking powder over the mixture and lightly stir in with a large metal

spoon to give a dropping consistency, when it falls easily from the spoon if given a medium flick.

3 Spoon into the pudding mold. Lay a disc of parchment paper on the pudding and cover the top of the mold. Put the mold in the saucepan of boiling water, cover the pan, and steam the pudding for about 1½ hours until lightly set in the center.

4 Remove the mold from the pan and leave to stand for a few minutes before unmolding on to a warm plate.

Scant 1 cup Pink Grapefruit Curd
1 stick unsalted butter, diced
Scant ½ cup superfine sugar
2 eggs, beaten
2 lemons, zested and juiced
1 cup self-rising flour
1 teaspoon baking powder

SERVES 4

Opposite: Pink grapefruit curd

Lemon and passionfruit curd

2 large lemons, zested and juiced
Scant 1 cup sugar
$\frac{1}{3}$ cup unsalted butter, diced
3 small eggs, beaten and strained
3 ripe passion fruit, seeds and pulp

MAKES ABOUT 1 $\frac{1}{2}$ CUPS

Homemade lemon curd is a great favorite with many people, but it does take a while to prepare, so few make it from scratch. I therefore know it will be a welcome gift. I like to add passionfruit to give it an extra special, exotic fragrance.

1 Put the lemon zest and juice, sugar, and butter in a heatproof bowl set over a pan of gently simmering water. Heat gently, stirring with a wooden spoon, until the sugar has dissolved and the butter has melted.

2 Stir in the eggs and continue to heat, stirring frequently at first, then constantly until the mixture is thick enough to coat the back of the spoon.

Do not allow the water in the pan to boil or the mixture will curdle.

3 Remove the bowl from the pan and stir in the passion fruit pulp and seeds. Pour or ladle the curd into warm, sterilized jars, seal, and leave to cool completely (see page 29). Label and store in the refrigerator for up to three months, unopened. Eat within three to four days once opened.

Moroccan preserved lemons

3 to 4 unwaxed, thin-skinned lemons
About $\frac{1}{4}$ cup kosher salt
3 to 4 bay leaves (optional)
Juice of 2 to 3 lemons

MAKES ABOUT 4 CUPS

Lemons preserved in salt are one of the hallmark foods of Morocco. To emulate as nearly as possible the taste of the freshly picked, sun-ripened lemons that are used in Morocco, take care when selecting the lemons you will use. Pick smooth, thin-skinned fruits with a rich, yellow color that are not too firm, and do not have large "knobs" on the end. (The lemons for sale in England, where I live, are almost invariably underripe, so I keep them for at least a few days at room temperature to soften them.) Before using the lemons, roll them firmly on the work surface to help release their juice. Use preserved lemons sparingly with chicken, fish dishes, and in bean and legume salads.

To use preserved lemons

Unless otherwise directed in a recipe, rinse the required number of lemons thoroughly in cold water, then cut away and discard the soft inner flesh. Thinly slice the rind and use as required. Thick-skinned lemons will need light cooking, but thin-skinned lemons can be used as is – as a garnish, for example.

1 Make slits or "pockets" on either side of each lemon by cutting downwards from the top to within $\frac{1}{2}$ inch of the base. Gently open each lemon and pack salt into the cuts. Reshape the lemons.

2 Spoon a layer of salt into a warm, sterilized jar, then pack the lemons into the jar, pressing them firmly and squeezing in as many as possible. Sprinkle in any remaining salt, and add the bay leaves, if using, as you go.

3 Add enough lemon juice to come within $\frac{1}{2}$ inch of the top of the jar. Cover with nonreactive lids. Label the jar and store in a cool, dark, dry place for at least one month before using. Keeps for one to two years.

Opposite: Moroccan preserved lemons

Nectarines in almond-flavored wine

12 ripe but firm nectarines
2¼ cups sugar
3 cups dry white wine
3 tablespoons almond liqueur
Brandy (see method)

MAKES 8 CUPS

While there is no need to use a really good wine for this recipe, I don't recommend using a thin, acidic one, either. I have experimented with different types of wine in this recipe, and as a change from the almond flavor, I like using a muscat dessert wine (any dessert wine from southern France would do) which has a fruity and sweet taste with enough underlying acidity to prevent it from being cloying.

1 Immerse the nectarines in a pan of gently boiling water for 20 to 30 seconds. Immediately transfer all the nectarines to a bowl of cold water. When cool enough to handle, remove the skins with a sharp knife or your fingers. Cut three or four of the nectarines in half and remove the pits. Crack the pits and take out the inner kernels.

2 Put the kernels, sugar, and wine in a saucepan and heat gently, stirring, until the sugar has dissolved. Heat just to the simmering point, and simmer gently for eight minutes.

3 Add the nectarines to the syrup, in batches if necessary, and poach five minutes for the halved fruit, 10 minutes for the whole fruit.

4 Using a slotted spoon, immediately transfer the nectarines to warm, sterilized jars.

5 When all the nectarines have been poached, boil the syrup for 10 minutes. Discard the kernels and add the almond liqueur. Pour the syrup evenly into the prepared jars (see page 11). Add brandy to top the jars off, and swirl them to expel any air bubbles, seal, and leave until cool (see page 17). Label and store in a cool, dark, dry place for two months before eating. Keeps for at least one year.

Almond-flavored nectarine puffs

1 lb puff pastry
⅔ cup mascarpone cheese
2½ Nectarines in Almond-Flavored Wine
  (see page 76), drained and chopped
1 egg
½ teaspoon sugar

SERVES 6

Partnering the luscious nectarines with puff pastry and voluptuous mascarpone cheese makes a wonderfully indulgent dessert for a winter dinner party. Puff pastry can be purchased from the frozen food section of supermarkets and grocery stores.

1 Place a cookie sheet in the refrigerator to chill. Roll out the pastry to about ¼ inch thick. Trim the edges with a large sharp knife, then cut into six squares.

2 Put a generous spoonful of mascarpone cheese into the center of each square. Divide the nectarines among the squares.

3 Dampen the corners of the pastry with water and bring them up to meet in the center. Press the edges together firmly to seal them. Transfer to a cold cookie sheet.

4 Beat the egg with the sugar and brush over the pastry, taking care not to get any egg on the seams. Put in the refrigerator for at least 30 minutes.

5 Preheat the oven to 400°F. Bake the puffs for 15 to 20 minutes until puffed and golden. Serve immediately.

Brandied peaches with Cointreau

3 to 4 lb ripe but firm peaches,
  depending on size, halved and pitted
1½ cups superfine sugar
1¼ cups Cointreau
About 2¼ cups brandy

MAKES ABOUT 10 CUPS

Cointreau is made on the outskirts of Angers, on the banks of the river Loire, France. Quite simply it is a mixture of dry bitter orange peels and fresh sweet orange peels, with beet sugar and alcohol.

1 Pack the peach halves into sterilized jars, sprinkling sugar between the layers as you go, to within 1 inch of the top.

2 Mix the Cointreau with 2 cups brandy and pour into prepared jars (see page 11). If necessary, top off with extra brandy so it comes to within ½ inch of the top. Swirl the jars to release any air bubbles.

3 Seal the jars (see page 37), label, and store in a cool, dark, dry place for at least three months before eating. Swirl the jars daily for the first one or two weeks to ensure the sugar dissolves. Keeps for 18 to 24 months.

Peach chutney

When I was working in southern France, there was such an abundance of wonderful fruit in the summer and early autumn that I decided to emulate my forebears and preserve some for the dreary winter back in England. The sight and smell of the preparation of the chutney aroused much astonishment among my French neighbors, who weren't very fond of the taste when it was first made. Fortunately, I stayed in France long enough for the flavor of the chutney to develop and mellow. When they finally tasted it, they admitted, rather grudgingly, that it wasn't bad, and they could see the reason for the chutney – for England and the English.

4 lb ripe but firm peaches, halved and pitted
2 tart cooking apples, cored and chopped
1$\frac{1}{2}$ cups chopped dried peaches
4 garlic cloves, chopped
1 teaspoon freshly grated nutmeg
1 tablespoon ground ginger
$\frac{1}{4}$ teaspoon cayenne pepper
2$\frac{1}{2}$ cups white wine vinegar
Scant 2 cups sugar

MAKES ABOUT 8 CUPS

1 Put all the ingredients except the sugar in a large nonreactive pan. Bring to a boil, then simmer gently for about 30 minutes until the fruit is soft.

2 Over low heat, stir in the sugar, then continue to simmer for approximately one hour until the chutney is thick and no liquid flows into the channel when the spoon is drawn across the bottom of the pan. It will thicken further upon standing.

3 Prepare and fill the jars (see page 11), then heat-process in a boiling-water canner (see page 14). Let cool. Label the jars and store in a cool, dark, dry place at least 6 to 8 weeks before eating. Keeps for up to 1 year.

Peach conserve

This recipe puts bruised or other slightly imperfect fruit to a very good use. Try to use a good quality brandy because the taste will be reflected in the conserve. You will need enough pieces of vanilla bean to correspond to the number of jars that are filled.

About 2$\frac{1}{2}$ lb just-ripe peaches
Juice of 2 lemons
3 cups preserving sugar
Small pat of unsalted butter
4 tablespoons brandy
1 to 2 vanilla beans, cut into 3 inch lengths

MAKES ABOUT 4 CUPS

1 Dip each peach in boiling water for 30 seconds, then peel off the skin . Cut the peaches in half and remove the pits. Cut away any bruised flesh. Chop the peaches.

2 Put the peaches in a nonreactive pan with the lemon juice and sugar. Cover and leave for a few hours, stirring occasionally.

3 Bring the contents of the pan to a boil, then cook gently for 15 to 20 minutes until the peaches are tender. Add the butter and boil hard, stirring frequently, for about 15 minutes until a soft setting point is reached (see page 23).

4 Remove from the heat and leave for 10 minutes. Stir in the brandy. Prepare and fill the jars (see page 11), inserting a piece of vanilla in each one. Heat-process in a boiling-water canner (see page 14). Leave to cool. Label the jars and store in a cool, dark, dry place for one month before eating. Use within six months.

Orange and ginger marmalade

True Spanish Seville oranges, the "ultimate" marmalade orange,
are only available in January and early to mid-February, so to make
marmalade with them, you must plan ahead and either use them right away,
or freeze them for later use. Even if I do manage this ideal, I don't always
buy enough fruit to make sufficient marmalade to last throughout the year.
When that happens, then out comes this recipe, a variation of traditional
orange marmalade, which calls for ordinary eating oranges paired with
lemons. A measure of whisky is also likely to find its way into the mixture
after the pan has been removed from the heat for the last time.

2 lb large oranges

2 small lemons

¼ cup fresh ginger, grated

10 cups water

4 lb granulated sugar or preserving sugar

MAKES ABOUT 12 CUPS

1 Cut the oranges and lemons in
half and squeeze, reserving the juice
and seeds. Remove the skin and
membranes from the fruit and,
along with the seeds, tie them in
a cheesecloth bag with a long
length of string.

2 Pour the orange and lemon juices
into a nonreactive pan with the
ginger and water. Tie the cheesecloth
bag to the handle of the pan so it is
suspended in the contents. Bring to
a boil and simmer gently for about
1½ hours, until the peel is tender
and the contents of the pan are
reduced by half.

3 Lift out the cheesecloth bag and
press it firmly against the side of
the pan to extract the liquid.
Discard the bag.

4 Stir the sugar into the pan and
heat gently, stirring, until the sugar
has dissolved. Increase the heat and
boil the marmalade hard for about
15 minutes until the setting point
is reached (see page 23).

5 Remove the pan from the heat and
skim any scum from the surface. Let
stand for about 10 minutes, then stir.
Prepare and fill the jars (see page 11),
then heat-process in a boiling-water
canner (see page 14). Leave to cool
before labeling and storing in a cool,
dark, dry place for up to one year.

"Candied" orange peel in honey

About 1¼ cups mixed citrus fruit peels
Water (see method)
About 2 cups honey

MAKES ABOUT 2½ CUPS

You can use a combination of citrus fruit peels along with the orange peel – grapefruit, lemon, and lime. I use this macerated peel in chocolate and fruit tarts, pies, compotes, and spooned over pancakes or ice cream.

1 Cut the fruit peel into strips according to the width and length that you like; I do a variety of sizes. Bring a saucepan of water to a boil. Add the peels, quickly return the water to a boil, and boil for four minutes. Drain into a colander or sieve and rinse under cold running water. Dry well with paper towels, then spread on a clean cloth on a wire rack and leave in a warmish, dry place to dry completely.

2 Put a layer of peels in a dry, sterilized jar and cover with honey. Repeat the layering until all the peel has been used. Insert a sterilized skewer or knitting needle into the jar to release any air bubbles.

3 Cover the jar tightly and leave in a cool, dark place for at least three months, checking occasionally to make sure that the peel is still covered by honey. Add more honey if necessary. Keeps for up to one year.

Orange rice gateau

¼ stick unsalted butter, diced
¼ cup arborio rice
Scant 1 cup muscat dessert wine
2½ cups half-and-half, or all whole milk
3 large eggs, separated
1½ tablespoons ground almonds
4 tablespoons chopped drained
  "Candied" Orange Peel in Honey

SERVES 4

This delightful, light, moist rice pudding "cake" has the rich taste of a honey-flavored dessert wine and is studded with "jewels" of bittersweet citrus peel. It can be served hot for dessert, perhaps accompanied by strawberries, raspberries or peaches, or left until cold and served with raspberry or apricot sauce.

1 Heat the butter in a nonstick saucepan, add the rice, and stir until the grains are well coated in butter. Pour in the wine and boil until it is almost evaporated. Add the half-and-half, or milk, bring to a boil, stir once, then simmer for about 30 minutes until thick and creamy and the rice is tender but still firm to the bite. Remove from the heat and leave to cool slightly. Meanwhile, preheat the oven to 325°F.

2 Beat the egg yolks and ground almonds into the cooked rice, then stir in the peel. Whisk the egg whites until stiff, then fold into the rice in three batches, using a large metal spoon.

3 Transfer to a greased 8-inch round baking dish (such as a soufflé dish), or cake pan with a removable bottom if the gateau is to be turned out. Bake for about one hour until golden and just firm to the touch in the center; take care not to overcook, otherwise it will be too dry. Leave the gateau to stand for about 10 minutes to firm up before unmolding, or serve immediately if not unmolding.

Orange rice gateau

Orange chutney

2½ cups white wine vinegar

2 slim cinnamon sticks

1½ tablespoons chopped fresh ginger

2 teaspoons allspice berries, crushed

1 teaspoon whole cloves

6 large, seedless oranges

1 onion, finely chopped

1 tart cooking apple, cored and
chopped without peeling

2 cups light brown sugar

1⅛ cup fresh dates, pitted and
chopped

MAKES 7 CUPS

I am not a fan of the lime pickle that is often
served as an accompaniment to Indian dishes,
so I like to offer this chutney instead.

1 Put the vinegar and spices in a nonreactive
saucepan, bring to a boil, then simmer for five to
10 minutes until the vinegar is flavored to your
liking, then strain.

2 Meanwhile, peel and coarsely chop the oranges,
discarding any seeds. Shred or finely chop the peel.
Add to the vinegar and leave to steep overnight.

3 Add the orange flesh, onion, and apple to the
vinegar and simmer until soft. Stir in the sugar until
it has dissolved, then add the dates and chopped
orange, and simmer steadily. The chutney is ready
when it is thick and no liquid appears in the
channel that is left when the spoon is drawn across
the bottom of the pan. The chutney will thicken
upon standing.

4 Remove the pan from the heat. Prepare and fill
the jars (see page 11), then heat-process in a boiling-
water canner (see page 14). Leave to cool. Label the
jars and store in a cool, dark, dry place for two
months before eating. Keep for up to one year.

Sweet pickled orange slices

Sweet pickled orange slices

It wouldn't be Christmas without a dish of sweet pickled orange slices to eat with leftover turkey and ham. It was part of my family's tradition that my grandmother prepared the oranges, as well as the Christmas pudding and the mincemeat.

1 Cut the oranges into ¼-inch thick slices. Put into a large nonreactive pan with just enough water to cover. Simmer gently for about 20 to 30 minutes until the rind of the slices is soft.

2 Lift the slices from the pan using a slotted spoon. Add the vinegar, sugar, spices, and lemon peel to the pan. Bring to a boil, then simmer for 10 minutes.

3 Return the orange slices to the pan and poach gently until the rind is semi-transparent. Using a slotted spoon, transfer the slices to warm, sterilized jars (see page 11), packing the slices neatly.

4 Boil the liquid that remains in the pan until it begins to thicken and become syrupy. Strain into the jars to cover the fruit by 1 inch, then heat-process in a boiling-water canner (see page 16). Cool, label, and store in a cool, dark, dry place for at least six weeks before eating. Keeps for up to one year.

6 large, thin-skinned oranges
Water to cover
3¾ cups white wine vinegar
3½ cups sugar
6 cloves
1 large cinnamon stick
2 star anise, crushed
Seeds from 5 cardamom pods, crushed
10 black peppercorns, crushed
Finely shredded peel of 1 lemon

MAKES ABOUT 8 CUPS

Clear tangerine marmalade

The total weight of the fruit should be about 3 lb. Because the fruit pith and seeds are removed when the marmalade is strained, there is no need to tie in a cheesecloth bag. Clementines or fresh mandarin oranges can also be used.

1 Peel the tangerines and finely shred the peel. Tie the peel in a cheesecloth bag with a long length of string. Peel the grapefruit and lemon, and chop the peel finely. Coarsely chop all of the fruit, reserving the juice and any seeds. Put the reserved juice and seeds, flesh, and grapefruit and lemon peel in a nonreactive pan with the water. Tie the cheesecloth bag to the handle of the pan so it is suspended in the contents.

2 Simmer gently for 1½ to 2 hours until the peel is soft. Remove the cheesecloth bag after 30 minutes and drain the contents of the bag through a sieve. Rinse this peel under cold running water, drain, and spread out on a clean cloth to air-dry.

3 Pour the contents of the pan into a jelly bag suspended over a nonreactive bowl and leave overnight in a cool place to drip.

4 Discard the pulp that remains in the jelly bag. Pour the juice into a clean pan and add the sugar and tangerine peel. Heat gently, stirring, until the sugar has dissolved, then boil hard for about 10 minutes until the setting point has been reached (see page 23).

5 Remove any scum with a slotted spoon, leave the marmalade to stand for 15 minutes, then stir. Prepare and fill the jars (see page 11), then heat-process in a boiling-water canner (see page 14). Cool, label the jars, and store in a cool, dark, dry place for up to one year.

2 lb tangerines
1 large grapefruit
1 lemon
10 cups water
6 cups granulated sugar or preserving sugar

MAKES ABOUT 10 CUPS

Pear and kiwi chutney

1½ lb ripe but firm pears, cored and chopped, but not peeled

1½ lb kiwi fruit, chopped with the peel on

1 packed cup chopped dried apricots

⅓ cup raisins

3 garlic cloves, finely chopped

2½ tablespoons finely chopped fresh ginger

1 to 2 teaspoons cayenne pepper, or to taste

1 tablespoon freshly ground coriander seeds

2 teaspoons kosher salt

1¼ cups cider vinegar

1 cup firmly packed soft light brown sugar

MAKES ABOUT 7 TO 8 CUPS

It is such a shame that kiwi fruit does not keep its attractive, emerald color when it is cooked. Instead of adding vibrancy to the appearance of the chutney, it just merges into the other ingredients. Use a well-flavored eating variety of pear such as Bosc or Bartlett.

1 Put all the ingredients except the brown sugar in a nonreactive saucepan. Cover and simmer for 15 minutes, stirring occasionally, until the pears and kiwi fruit are soft.

2 Stir in the sugar until it has dissolved, then bring to a boil. Simmer gently until the chutney is thick and no liquid flows into the channel when the spoon is drawn across the bottom of the pan. Remember, the chutney will thicken upon standing.

3 Prepare the jars and fill (see page 11), then heat-process in a boiling-water canner (see page 14). Let cool, label, and store in a cool, dark, dry place at least 6 to 8 weeks before eating. Keeps for up to one year.

Mulled pears

3 lb small, slightly underripe pear pieces

Whole cloves (see method)

3 inch cinnamon stick, broken into piece

2 blades of mace

3-inch piece fresh ginger, chopped

Peel of 1 lemon, cut into strips

1 cup plus 2 tablespoons sugar

About ¾ bottle red wine

MAKES ABOUT TWO 4-CUP PLUS ONE 2¼-CUP WIDE-MOUTHED JARS

The pears should not be rock hard, so, if necessary, leave them at room temperature for a few days until they are just beginning to "give" when gently pressed. A soft, fruity wine, such as a Chinon (a French red wine from the Loire region) a Beaujolais, or a merlot-based wine is more suitable for use in this recipe than something made from cabernet sauvignon grapes, which is more robust.

1 Carefully peel the pears, leaving the stems intact. Stud each pear with a clove, then divide among two 4-cup and one 2¼-cup jars (see page 11). Distribute the remaining spices evenly among the jars.

2 Gently heat the sugar in the wine until it has dissolved, then heat until the wine is hot but not boiling.

3 Pour the wine into the sterilized jars to come within ½ inch of the top. Process in a boiling-water canner (see page 16).

Opposite: Pear and kiwi chutney

Plum jam

2½ lb plums, halved
1¼ cups water
4½ cups granulated sugar or
  preserving sugar
Pat of unsalted butter

MAKES ABOUT 4 CUPS

The color of this jam will vary depending on the type of plums used. Red-fleshed plums produce a richly red jam, while green-fleshed plums like greengages or Italian plums make for a greenish-yellow jam. If the plums are large, cut them into quarters rather than halves.

1 Put the plums in a nonreactive pan and add the water. Bring to a boil, then simmer for about 25 to 30 minutes, stirring occasionally, until the plum skins are soft and the fruit is really tender. The liquid should be well reduced.

2 Stir in the sugar until dissolved. Add the butter and bring the jam to a boil. Boil rapidly for about 10 to 15 minutes until the setting point is reached (see page 23).

3 Remove the pan from the heat, remove the pits and any scum from the surface with a slotted spoon, and let stand for about five minutes. Stir the jam gently and remove from the heat.

4 Prepare and fill the jars (see page 11), and heat-process in a boiling-water canner (see page 14). Let cool, label, and store in a cool, dark dry place for one month before eating. Keeps for up to two years.

Plum and walnut conserve

4 lb plums
1¼ cups water
2 slim cinnamon sticks
7 cups preserving sugar
1 cup walnut halves, chopped
4 tablespoons brandy

MAKES 9½ CUPS

The addition of walnuts adds an interesting texture contrast to this conserve. Yet more interest comes from the subtle flavor of cinnamon plus a dash of brandy. For best results, use freshly brought walnut halves (or better still, use whole nuts in the shell) and chop them yourself, because the ready-chopped nuts are usually an inferior quality.

1 Halve the plums and put the stones in a small saucepan with the water. Bring to a boil, then simmer for 10 minutes. Strain off the water and discard the stones.

2 Put the plums, cinnamon sticks, and flavored water in a nonreactive pan and cook gently for about 10 minutes until the plums have softened.

3 Stir in the sugar until it has dissolved, then bring to a boil and boil for 10 to 20 minutes until the setting point is reached (see page 23).

4 Remove the pan from the heat and stir in the walnuts and brandy. Stand for five minutes, scoop out the cinnamon sticks, and stir gently. Prepare and fill the jars (see page 11), then heat-process in a boiling-water canner (see page 14). Let cool, label, and store in a cool, dark, dry place for one month before eating.

Spiced plum sauce

This is a traditional, Western plum sauce that used to be popularly served in England with cold meats, particularly game, game pies, and pâtés.

1 Tie the coriander, cloves, anise, and cinnamon in a cheesecloth bag using a long length of string. Put the remaining ingredients except the sugar into a nonreactive pan. Tie the cheesecloth bag to the handle of the pan so the bag is suspended in the contents. Bring to a boil, then simmer, stirring occasionally, for about 45 minutes.

2 Over low heat, stir in the sugar until dissolved, then continue to simmer gently for another 45 minutes until the sauce is reduced to a heavy pulp.

3 Lift out the cheesecloth bag and press it firmly against the side of the pan to extract the liquid. Discard the bag.

4 Strain the contents of the pan through a colander to remove the pits and skin. For a smoother sauce, pass it through a nonreactive fine sieve.

5 Return the sauce to a clean pan and bring to a boil; continue to boil the sauce to further reduce it if it is too runny. Pour into warm, sterilized, dry bottles to come to the top (see page 11), and process in a boiling-water canner (see page 16). Let cool, label, and store in a cool, dark, dry place for at least one month before eating. Use within six months.

10 coriander seeds, crushed
4 whole cloves
3 star anise, crushed
1 cinnamon stick
2½ cups red wine vinegar
3 lb red or purple plums, chopped
1 small onion, chopped
3 large garlic cloves, chopped
2¾ cups light brown sugar

MAKES 7 CUPS

Lamb spirals with plum sauce and bok choy

8 boneless lamb steaks, each
  weighing about ¼ lb
Freshly ground black pepper to taste
6-8 tablespoons Spiced Plum Sauce
  (see page 91)
Peanut oil, for frying
3 garlic cloves, chopped
3 tablespoons finely
  chopped fresh ginger
1 lb bok choy, shredded
3 tablespoons sesame oil
4 large scallions, chopped
3 tablespoons cashew nuts
Salt to taste

SERVES 4

Although very different from the Chinese
version of plum sauce, the English sauce is
just as useful in cooking (in fact, I prefer it),
and I have used it for a Chinese-style dish.

1 In turn, lay the lamb steaks between 2 sheets
of parchment paper and, using a meat cleaver
or rolling pin, pound them until they are thin.
Remove the paper.

2 Season the flattened steaks with black pepper,
and spread the plum sauce over the meat, being
careful not to take it to the edges. Roll up the
steaks and secure with wooden toothpicks.

3 Heat a little oil in a skillet, add the lamb
rolls, and fry over a medium heat until the lamb
is browned and cooked through to your liking,
about 10 to 20 minutes. Turn frequently to
ensure even cooking. Transfer to a warm plate,
cover, and keep warm.

4 Add a little more oil to the pan, heat,
and then add the garlic and ginger. Stir-fry,
stirring frequently, for two to three
minutes until fragrant.

5 Increase the heat, add the bok choy, and stir-
fry until it begins to wilt. Add the sesame oil,
spring onions, and cashew nuts and continue
to stir-fry for a couple of minutes.

6 Transfer to four serving plates, sprinkle salt
over the lamb, and add two rolls to each plate.

Freezer raspberry jam

$\frac{1}{2}$ lb raspberries
4$\frac{1}{2}$ cups superfine sugar
$\frac{1}{2}$ cup liquid pectin

MAKES 7 CUPS

Freezer jams are not boiled, so they have a fresher, more natural taste and a brighter, clearer color than cooked jams. For a change, instead of using ordinary superfine sugar, try using vanilla sugar, which can be bought or made on your own. Simply insert a vanilla bean in a jar of sugar and leave for two weeks before using; the vanilla bean can be left in the jar, or used in another recipe.

1 Place the raspberries in a bowl and gently stir the sugar using a fork, and lightly mashing the berries. Leave for 20 minutes, stirring occasionally.

2 Pour in the liquid pectin and stir constantly for three minutes.

3 Ladle the jam into clean, freezer-proof containers filling them to $\frac{1}{2}$ inch from the top. Seal. Label and let cool for about five hours.

4 Put the jam in the refrigerator and leave for 24 to 48 hours until it gels.

5 Put the jam in the freezer and store for up to six months.

6 To serve, leave at room temperature for about one hour, depending on the size of the container.

Raspberry and pear jelly

2 lb just ripe pears, very finely chopped
1 cup fruit juice, such as grape or
   unsweetened apple
2 lb raspberries
Granulated sugar (see method)
Commercial pectin (see method)

MAKES ABOUT 4 CUPS

Raspberries and pears go very well together in terms of flavor, but they are not ideal partners in producing a well-set jelly because they are both low in pectin. In a case such as this, jam sugar comes to the rescue.

1 Put the pears in a nonreactive pan, add the fruit juice, and simmer until the pears are tender, stirring occasionally too ensure even cooking.

2 Stir the raspberries into the pan, squash them with a potato masher, and heat gently until the juices of the berries have run.

3 Pour the contents of the pan into a jelly bag suspended over a nonreactive bowl and leave overnight in a cool place to drip.

4 Discard the pulp that is left in the jelly bag. Measure the juice into a clean pan. For each 2$\frac{1}{2}$ cups juice, stir

2 cups plus 2 tablespoons sugar into the pan, and add pectin according to the manufacturer's instructions. Heat gently, stirring, until the sugar has dissolved, then boil until the setting point is reached (see page 23).

5 Skim any scum from the surface with a slotted spoon. Prepare the jars and fill (see page 11), then heat-process in a boiling-water canner (see page 14). Leave in a cold place overnight. Label the jars and store in a cool, dark, dry place for up to six months.

Opposite: Raspberry and pear jelly

Raspberry and red currant jam

Raspberries are low in pectin, while red currants are a rich source, and combining them not only makes a delicious jam but also solves any setting problems. Because red currants can be difficult to find in the United States, you may want to substitute another tart berry that is high in pectin, such as gooseberries.

2 lb raspberries
1 lb red currants, stripped from their stalks
Juice of 1 lemon
7 cups granulated sugar or preserving sugar
Pat of butter (optional)

MAKES 6 CUPS

1 Put half the raspberries and all the red currants in a nonreactive pan and cook over a very low heat until the juices run, stirring gently, if necessary.

2 Add the remaining raspberries, lemon juice, and sugar to the pan. Heat gently, stirring, to dissolve the sugar, then increase the heat and boil for about 15 minutes until the setting point is reached (see page 23). Add the butter if scum formation is a problem.

3 Remove from the heat and let stand for 10 minutes. Prepare the jars and fill (see page 11), then heat-process in a boiling-water canner (see page 14). Let cool, label the jars, and store in a cool, dark, dry place for up to one year.

Raspberry syrup

3 lb ripe raspberries
Juice of 2 lemons
Sugar (see method)

MAKES 4 1/3 CUPS

Making a fruit syrup is a good use for surplus fruit that is too ripe to turn into successful jams or jellies. Instead of being processed in a boiling-water canner, the syrup can simply be kept in the fridge for three to four weeks, or frozen in ice-cube trays. Remove the frozen cubes from the trays, place into plastic bags, and return to the freezer. As well as being used as the basis for drinks, both soft and alcoholic, the syrup can be used to dress-up desserts.

1 Put the raspberries in a large heatproof bowl and place the bowl over a saucepan of simmering water. Heat the raspberries, stirring occasionally, until warmed and the juices begin to run. Pour through a nylon sieve lined with a double thickness of cheesecloth, and press gently with a wooden spoon to extract as much juice as possible.

2 Measure the juice. For every 2 1/2 cups juice, put 1 cup firmly packed sugar into a nonreactive saucepan. Add the juice and heat gently, stirring, until the sugar has dissolved. Add the lemon juice and leave to cool for 5 minutes.

3 Pour the syrup into sterilized bottles (see page 11) to within 1/2 inch of the top. Wipe the rim.

4 Heat-process in a boiling-water canner (see page 16). Label the bottles and store in a cool, dark, dry place for up to six months.

Raspberry, peach, and amaretto sundaes

3 large, ripe peaches, chopped
8 amaretto or small almond cookies, crushed
1 1/2 cups crème fraîche
About 3/4 to 1 cup Raspberry Syrup

SERVES 4

Vanilla ice cream or frozen yogurt can be used instead of crème fraîche; serve the sundaes immediately after assembling.

1 Mix the peaches with the amaretto cookies. Divide half the mixture among four tall glasses.

2 Spoon half the crème fraîche into the glasses, and spoon half the syrup over the crème fraîche.

3 Repeat the layering. Leave to stand for at least 30 minutes before serving.

Opposite: Raspberry, peach, and amaretto sundaes

Rhubarb and orange marmalade

Rosy rhubarb jam

Pink rather than green rhubarb will produce the jam with the best color. If you have green rhubarb, or instead of using roses, try adding five finely shredded fresh angelica leaves instead, which adds a sweet fragrance to the jam. Refer to page 145 for the selection of the rose petals.

1 Put the rhubarb, rose petals, and sugar in a nonmetallic bowl. Stir well, cover, and leave in a cool place overnight.

2 The next day, transfer the contents of the bowl to a nonreactive pan, add the lemon juice, and heat gently, stirring, until the sugar has dissolved. Increase the heat and bring to a boil, then boil for about 15 minutes, stirring as necessary, until the setting point is reached (see page 23).

3 Remove from the heat and skim any scum from the surface. Stand for 10 minutes. Prepare and fill the jars (see page 11). Heat-process in a boiling-water canner (see page 14). Leave overnight. Label the jars and store in a cool, dark, dry place for at least two weeks. Use within six months.

2 lb rhubarb, sliced
Good handful of dark red, fragrant
  rose petals, torn into shreds
2 lb granulated sugar or preserving sugar
Juice of 1 lemon

MAKES ABOUT 6 CUPS

Rhubarb and orange marmalade

For the best flavor and to keep the boiling time after the addition of the rhubarb, use small or medium-sized rhubarb rather then long, thick ones which contain more water than taste.

1 Thinly pare the peel from the oranges and lemons. Finely shred the peel.

2 Squeeze the juice from the oranges and lemons, reserving the seeds, and pour into a nonreactive pan. Chop the pith and membrane finely and, along with the seeds, tie in a cheesecloth bag with a long length of string. Add the shredded peel and water to the pan. Tie the cheesecloth bag to the handle of the pan so it is suspended in the contents. Simmer gently for about 15 minutes until the peel has softened to your taste.

3 Add the rhubarb to the pan and cook gently until the fruit becomes a thick pulp.

4 Remove the cheesecloth bag and press it firmly against the side of the pan to extract the liquid. Stir in the sugar and heat gently, stirring, until the sugar has dissolved, then boil hard for about 10 minutes until the setting point has been reached (see page 23).

5 Remove any scum from the surface with a slotted spoon, and let the marmalade stand 15 minutes. Stir to distribute the peel. Prepare and fill the jars (see page 11), then heat-process in a boiling-water canner (see page 14). Leave overnight to cool. Label the jars and store in a cool, dark, dry place for up to nine to 12 months.

2 large oranges
2 lemons
2 cups water
3 lb rhubarb, cut into short lengths
6 cups granulated sugar or
  preserving sugar

MAKES 9 CUPS

Strawberry syrup

For a well-flavored syrup, use ripe, tasty strawberries; fruit that comes from the end of the season often has the best flavor. I have found that freshly picked berries taste better if they are left for a day in a cool place (the fridge if necessary) before eating or using. As well as serving this syrup as a drink, it can also be used as a sauce over ice cream, pancakes, or fresh fruit such as peaches, pears, or even strawberries.

3 lb ripe strawberries
Sugar (see method)
Juice of 2 lemons

MAKES 4⅓ CUPS

1 Puree the strawberries in a blender or food processor. Pour the puree into a nonreactive sieve lined with a double thickness of cheesecloth. Gather up the corners of the cheesecloth and press gently to extract as much juice as possible.

2 Measure the juice. For each 2½ cups juice, put 1 firmly packed cup sugar into a nonreactive saucepan. Heat the mixture gently,

stirring, until the sugar has dissolved. Add the lemon juice and leave to cool for five minutes.

3 Prepare the bottles (see page 11). Pour the syrup into sterilized bottles to within ½ inch of the top.

4 Process in a boiling-water canner (see page 16). Store in a cool, dark, dry place for up to six months.

Strawberry jam

I should think that strawberry jam is the most popular jam, and here are some secrets for making a good one. Use well-flavored fruit, and do not wash them; if the berries are dirty, try to clean them with a damp cloth or paper towel. More fruit than sugar should be used, and you can boost the pectin level by adding lemon juice, liquid pectin, or jam sugar, which also helps to give a good, fresh, fruity flavor because it reduces cooking time.

4½ lb strawberries, with hulls removed
8 cups granulated sugar
Commercial pectin (follow manufacturer's instructions for quantity and method)

MAKES ABOUT 10 CUPS

1 Cut large strawberries in half to speed the cooking. Layer the berries and sugar and pectin in a nonreactive bowl, cover, and leave overnight.

2 The next day, pour the contents of the bowl into a nonreactive pan and heat gently until the juices run, then simmer gently until the fruit is soft.

3 Bring to a boil, then simmer for about four minutes until the setting point is reached (see page 23).

4 Remove the pan from the heat and skim any scum from the surface with a slotted spoon. Let stand for about 10 minutes, then stir. Prepare and fill the jars (see page 11), then heat-process in a boiling-water canner (see page 14). Leave to cool, label the jars, and store them in a cool, dark, dry place for up to six months.

Opposite: Strawberry syrup

Summer berry jam

2½ lb mixed berries, such as strawberries, raspberries, red currants, and blueberries
4 cups granulated or preserving sugar
Juice of 2 lemons

MAKES 7 CUPS

Capture the true essence of summer by using your favorite sun-ripened, summer berries in this lovely jam. Although they are not berries, cherries can also be included, but weigh them after pitting.

1 Layer the fruit and sugar in a nonreactive bowl. Pour the lemon juice over the fruit. Cover and leave in a cool place until the sugar has dissolved, about eight hours.

2 Pour the contents of the bowl into a nonreactive pan. Heat gently until the juices are freely flowing.

3 Bring to a boil, then simmer until the setting point is reached (see page 23).

4 Remove the pan from the heat and skim any scum from the surface with a slotted spoon. Let stand for about 10 minutes. Stir. Prepare and fill the jars (see page 11), then heat-process in a boiling-water canner (see page 14). Let cool, label, and store in a cool, dark, dry place for up to six months.

Queen of puddings

2½ cups milk
1 large lemon, zested and juiced
3 medium eggs, separated
1 firmly packed cup superfine sugar
2 cups brioche, broken into coarse crumbs
9 tablespoons Summer Berry Jam, warmed

SERVES 6

Using a special, summery, homemade jam and buttery brioche crumbs, and cooking the puddings in individual dishes, turns this family favorite into a dessert that could grace any dinner party table.

1 Preheat the oven to 325°F. Heat the milk with the lemon zest in a saucepan, preferably nonstick, until it comes to a boil.

2 Meanwhile, whisk the egg yolks and ¼ cup of the sugar until thick and pale. Gradually whisk in the hot, flavored milk. Stir in the brioche crumbs.

3 Put six 1-cup ramekin dishes in a roasting pan and divide the custard among them. Bring the pan over to the oven, place on the oven rack, and pour boiling water into the pan to

come halfway up the sides of the dishes. Bake for 30 minutes until just set.

4 Remove the ramekins from the oven and brush the warmed jam liberally over the top of each pudding. Transfer to a broiler pan. Preheat the broiler.

5 Whisk the egg whites until stiff but not dry. Gradually whisk in the remaining sugar to make a meringue. Spoon on top of the jam, taking the meringue right to the edges of the dishes. Broil for 1 to 2 minutes until golden. Serve immediately.

Opposite: Queen of puddings

Pickled beets

When washing the beets, take care not to damage their skins. I usually dice the beets after roasting them, but they can be sliced if you prefer. If you are lucky enough to have baby beets, these can be pickled whole; reduce their baking time to about $1\frac{1}{2}$ to $1\frac{3}{4}$ hours.

1 Preheat the oven to 350°F. Wrap the beets in foil and bake in the oven for two to three hours, depending on size, until tender. Remove the beets from the oven and let cool.

2 Peel off and discard the beet skins, then dice them. Pack into sterilized jars, adding the horseradish, if using.

3 Add the salt to the vinegar; make sure it has dissolved. Bring to a boil in a nonreactive pan and pour over the beets to cover by $\frac{1}{2}$ inch. Swirl the jars to disperse any air bubbles.

4 Seal the jars, then label and store in a cool, dark, dry place for two months before eating. Keep for up to two years.

2 lb raw beets, tops removed
1 teaspoon grated raw horseradish, (optional)
1 teaspoon kosher salt
5 cups Spiced Vinegar (see page 38)

MAKES ABOUT 2 LB

Beet relish

I include some malt vinegar in this relish because its sharpness is needed to counteract the sweetness of the beets. If using pre-cooked beets, simply omit the first step.

1 Wrap the beets in foil and bake in a preheated oven at 350°F for two to three hours, until soft. Remove the beets from oven and let cool. Peel off and discard the beet skins.

2 Meanwhile, put the onion and apples in a nonreactive pan. Add the red wine vinegar and malt vinegar. Bring to a boil, then simmer, stirring occasionally, for about 20 minutes until the onion and apple is tender.

3 Chop the beets and add to the pan along with the horseradish, brown sugar, and raisins. Heat gently, stirring, until the sugar has dissolved, then simmer for about 10 minutes until the relish has thickened. It will thicken further upon standing.

4 Prepare and fill the jars (see page 11), then heat-process in a boiling-water canner (see page 14). Leave to cool, label, and store in a cool, dark, dry place for six weeks before eating. Keep for up to one year.

1 lb raw beets
1 red onion, thinly sliced
2 tart cooking apples, cored and sliced
$\frac{1}{2}$ cup red wine vinegar
$\frac{1}{2}$ cup malt vinegar
4 tablespoons horseradish relish
$\frac{1}{3}$ cup light brown sugar
$\frac{1}{3}$ cup raisins

MAKES 2 LB

Opposite: Pickled beets

Grilled red peppers in oil

2 lb large, red bell peppers, halved, cored, and deseeded

1 red onion, finely chopped

Kosher salt (see method)

2 Oven-dried Tomatoes with Herbs (see page 133), cut into fine strips

About 3 small bay leaves

3 fresh thyme sprigs

2 tablespoons salt-packed capers

About 1½ cups olive oil, plus extra for brushing

MAKES 5 CUPS

Use peppers that feel heavy for their size because these will be the fleshiest. Grilling the peppers gives them an enticing, smoky flavor. Pitted black olives can also be added to the jars, if you like.

1 Layer the peppers and onions in a nonreactive bowl, sprinkling salt generously between the layers. Put a plate on top to press the vegetables lightly and leave in a cool place for one day, gently stirring occasionally.

2 Pour the peppers and onion into a colander and rinse under cold running water. Drain, dry with a clean cloth, and spread out on a dry, clean cloth to air-dry completely.

3 Preheat the grill or broiler. Reserving the red onion, brush the pepper halves with olive oil and cook on both sides until lightly charred and blistered.

4 Pack the peppers into a sterilized jar with the red onion, dried tomato strips, bay leaves, thyme, and capers.

5 Pour the oil into the jar so the peppers are completely covered. Swirl the jars to expel any trapped air bubbles, and seal. Leave in a cool, dark, dry place for at least one month before eating. Store for up to one year.

Pasta with peppers and prosciutto

14 or 16 oz packet dried fettuccine

6 halves Grilled Red Peppers in Oil, drained and cut into strips

About ½ lb prosciutto, cut into fine strips

About 2 tablespoons salt-packed capers

About 4 tablespoons fresh basil, cut into strips

4 tablespoons oil from the Grilled Red Peppers in Oil

Salt and freshly ground black pepper

SERVES 3 TO 4

The sight of a jar of intensely red Grilled Peppers in Oil provided the spark to my imagination one evening when I was feeling too tired to think of something quick to make for dinner. For a texture contrast, the prosciutto strips can be fried in a heavy skillet (without any added oil) until crisp before being tossed with the pasta.

1 Add the fettuccine to a large pan of boiling, salted water. Return quickly to the boil and boil according to the instructions on the packet.

2 Drain the pasta and toss with the remaining ingredients. Serve immediately.

Pasta with peppers and prosciutto

Provençal gratin

Homemade preserves come in handy for adding the little touches that instantly turn otherwise straightforward dishes into something special.

1 Preheat the oven to 425°F. If using a fresh red pepper, preheat the broiler. Broil the pepper until charred. If you prefer, let the pepper cool enough to handle, then peel off the skin. Slice the pepper.

2 Arrange the potato, zucchini, tomato, and red pepper in a layer in a large, shallow baking dish. Sprinkle with olives, cheese, herbs, salt, and plenty of black pepper. Repeat the layers, and end with layer of potato, cheese, and black pepper. Drizzle oil over the top.

3 Bake for 30 to 40 minutes until the top is brown and crisp.

2 halves Grilled Red Peppers in Oil (see page 108), sliced, or 1 small red pepper, halved lengthwise (optional)

2 lb waxy potatoes, boiled and thinly sliced

About ½ lb zucchini, thinly sliced

¾ lb tomatoes, sliced

About 12 pitted black olives, preferably oil-packed, chopped

2 oz piece of Parmesan cheese, grated

5 tablespoons chopped frozen Provençal herb blend (see page 57)

Salt and freshly ground black pepper to taste

Extra virgin olive oil, for drizzling

SERVES 4

Red pepper jelly

4 large red bell peppers, finely chopped

2 to 3 fresh red chile peppers, deseeded if liked, and finely chopped

1¾ cups cider vinegar

5 cups granulated sugar

Commercial pectin (follow manufacturer's instructions for quantity and method)

½ teaspoon kosher salt

MAKES ABOUT 4 CUPS

The fine chopping of the peppers for this clear, light ruby jelly is best done using a large, sharp knife, or mezzaluna, if you have one. Reserve any juices that come from chopping the peppers, and add them to the pan in Step 1. This preserve is both piquant and sweet, ideal for serving with, or glazing, roast or grilled chicken or pork, or for serving with soft, creamy cheeses.

1 Put the bell peppers, chile peppers, and vinegar in a nonreactive pan. Bring to a boil, then simmer for 15 minutes.

2 Pour the contents of the pan into a jelly bag suspended over a nonreactive bowl. Leave to drip for 15 minutes.

3 Discard the pulp left in the jelly bag. Pour the juice into a clean pan, stir in the sugar, pectin, and salt, and heat

gently, stirring, until the sugar has dissolved. Bring to a boil and simmer until the setting point is reached (see page 23).

4 Prepare and fill the jars (see page 11), then heat-process in a boiling-water canner (see page 14). Let cool. Label the jars and store in a cool, dark, dry place for up to six months.

Red pepper chutney

2¼ lb large, red bell peppers, chopped

1¼ lb red onions, chopped

1¼ lb tart cooking apples, cored and chopped

2 lb ripe but firm tomatoes, cored and chopped

3¾ cups red wine vinegar

2 tablespoons paprika

4 tablespoons grated fresh ginger

2 heaping teaspoons allspice berries, crushed

Pinch of crushed red pepper

2⅓ cups sugar

MAKES ABOUT 6 LB

To get the full benefit of the bright red color of the peppers, do not substitute light brown sugar for granulated sugar, even if you prefer the taste.

1 Put the red peppers, onions, apples, tomatoes, and vinegar in a nonreactive pan.

2 Tie the spices in a cheesecloth bag with a long length of string. Tie the end of the string to the handle of the pan so the bag is suspended in the contents. Boil gently for about 20 minutes until the vegetables and apples are tender.

3 Over low heat, stir in the sugar until it has dissolved, then simmer until thick. Squeeze the contents of

the cheesecloth bag against the side of the pan and remove the bag. The chutney is ready when no liquid appears in the channel left when a spoon is drawn through it. It will thicken further upon standing.

4 Prepare and fill the jars (see page 11), then heat-process in a boiling-water canner (see page 14). Let cool. Label the jars and store in a cool, dark, dry place for six weeks before eating. Keeps for up to one year.

Opposite: Red pepper jelly

Pickled red cabbage with orange

This preserve is best eaten within three to four months after it is made, as the cabbage softens upon storage. It goes well with bread and cheese, smoked meats, and casseroles.

1 Layer the cabbage and onion in a colander, sprinkling salt between each layer. Stand the colander on a plate and leave in a cool place overnight to drain. The next day, rinse the vegetables well, and dry thoroughly with a clean cloth. Spread out on another dry, clean cloth and let air-dry completely.

2 Meanwhile, make the spiced vinegar: put all the ingredients, and the orange rind and juice in a nonreactive pan and heat gently, stirring with a wooden spoon, until the sugar has dissolved, then boil for 2 minutes. Remove from the heat and leave to cool.

3 Return the vinegar to a boil; remove from the heat. Mix the raisins with the cabbage and onion and pack firmly into sterilized jars. Add the vinegar as you go, distributing the raisins and flavorings evenly, and pressing down firmly on the cabbage. Swirl the jars to expel any air bubbles. Seal the jars and let cool. Label the jars and store in a cool, dark, dry place for at least one month before eating. It will keep for up to one year but is best eaten with in three to four months.

1 red cabbage weighing about 2 lb, quartered, cored, and shredded
1 large onion, thinly sliced
Kosher salt
3 large oranges, zested and juiced

For the spiced vinegar:
1½ cups red wine vinegar
¾ cup raspberry vinegar
1½ teaspoons whole allspice berries, lightly crushed
1½ teaspoons black peppercorns
1½ teaspoons whole cloves
2 bay leaves, torn in half
2-inch long cinnamon stick
1 tablespoon brown sugar
½ cup raisins

MAKES ABOUT 2 LB

Pork braised with pickled red cabbage

This is a very easy recipe that is simple to make. Once the chops have been browned, the one-dish meal of cabbage, plums, and pork chops cooks happily without much attention from the cook. It will also wait without spoiling if you are not ready to eat at the end of its cooking time. If more convenient, the dish can also be cooked in a low oven, 300 to 325°F.

1 Quickly brown the pork chops on both sides in a skillet over a medium to high heat. Season with salt and pepper to taste, and transfer to a plate. Add the cabbage to the skillet to heat through.

2 Transfer the cabbage to a large, heavy, ovenproof casserole dish. Nestle the plums in the cabbage, and put the chops on top in a single layer. Cover the casserole and cook over a very low heat for about 45 minutes until the pork is very tender and the cabbage has softened. Turn the chops over halfway through cooking.

4 pork loin chops, weighing about ½ lb each
Salt and freshly ground black pepper to taste
1½ lb Pickled Red Cabbage with Orange, drained
4 ripe plums, about ¼ lb each, quartered and pitted

SERVES 4

Opposite: Pork braised with pickled red cabbage

Bread-and-butter pickles

2 small cucumbers, total weight
about 1 lb, sliced

1 Spanish onion, or other large,
mild onion, sliced

3 tablespoons kosher salt

¾ cup white wine vinegar

⅔ cup granulated sugar or light brown
sugar

2 teaspoons black mustard seed, lightly
crushed

1 teaspoon coriander seed, lightly
crushed

1 teaspoon celery seed, lightly crushed

Although often considered a classic American pickle, the original recipe for bread-and-butter pickles came from England. It has developed over the years to become the much-loved, sweet-and-sour preserve that we use today in sandwiches, as an accompaniment to hot dogs, and with innumerable other dishes.

1 Layer the cucumber and onion slices in a colander, sprinkling salt between each layer. Stand the colander on a plate and leave in a cool place overnight to drain. The next day, rinse the vegetables well, and dry thoroughly with a clean cloth.

2 Put the vinegar, sugar, mustard, coriander, and celery seeds in a nonreactive pan and heat gently, stirring with a wooden spoon, until the sugar has dissolved, then boil for three minutes.

3 Add the cucumber and onion to the pan, quickly return to the boil. Boil for one minute, then remove the pan from the heat.

4 Pack the vegetables in warm, sterilized jars and pour in enough hot vinegar to cover. Swirl the jars to expel any air bubbles, seal, and let cool. Label the jars and store in a cool, dark, dry place for one month before eating. Keeps for up to one year

Dill pickles

3 cups white wine vinegar

2½ cups water

1 teaspoon dill seeds

2 teaspoons black peppercorns, crushed

1 blade of mace (optional)

6 tablespoons kosher salt

10 to 12 small pickling cucumbers

1 bunch of fresh dill

4 to 5 large garlic cloves

MAKES ABOUT 3½ PINTS

This recipe uses a mixture of white wine vinegar and water to make a mild tasting pickle, which also means that these pickles must be kept in the fridge. Be sure to choose cucumbers that are unwaxed; otherwise the vinegar won't be able to penetrate the cucumber skin.

1 Pour the vinegar and water into a nonreactive pan. Add the dill seeds, peppercorns, mace, and salt. Bring to a boil over a high heat and boil hard for three minutes. Remove the pan from the heat and let cool.

2 Pack the cucumbers into a clean jar, adding the fresh dill and garlic as you go.

3 Pour the cold pickling liquid, including the spices, into the jar to fill. Seal the jar. Label the dill pickles

and store in the refrigerator. Check the cucumbers after a couple of days to ensure they are still covered by the pickling liquid. If they are not, put some crumpled greaseproof paper into the jar to hold the cucumbers down. Remove the paper after two weeks.

4 Store in the refrigerator for one month before eating. The cucumbers can be kept in the refrigerator for up to three months in total.

Opposite: Bread-and-butter pickles

Mediterranean chutney

2 lb large tomatoes, cored and chopped
¾ lb zucchini, chopped
¾ lb eggplant, chopped
1½ lb red bell pepper, chopped
¾ lb onion, chopped
3 garlic cloves, chopped
1 tablespoon paprika
1¼ tablespoons coriander seed, lightly crushed
1 tablespoon kosher salt
1¼ cups red wine vinegar
2 cups brown sugar

MAKES ABOUT 4 LB

Containing tomatoes, peppers, zucchini, and eggplant, this chutney should appeal to lovers of ratatouille. The proportions of the vegetables can be varied to suit your taste or to what you have available.

1 Gently heat all the vegetables, garlic, spices, and salt in a covered, large, nonreactive pan for about 10 minutes until the juices run, stirring occasionally.

2 Uncover the pan, bring to a boil, and simmer for about one hour until the vegetables are tender and most of the liquid has evaporated. Stir to prevent the vegetables from sticking.

3 Over low heat, stir in the vinegar and sugar until the sugar has

dissolved, and continue simmering. The chutney is ready when no liquid appears in the channel left when a spoon is drawn across the bottom of the pan. It will thicken further upon standing.

4 Prepare and fill the jars (see page 11), then heat-process in a boiling-water canner (see page 14). Store in a cool, dark, dry place for at least one month before eating. The chutney will keep for up to one year.

Pickled green beans

¾ lb large onions, thinly sliced
2 cups white wine vinegar
1 lb trimmed weight of green beans, sliced
Salt (see method)
7 teaspoons cornstarch
2 teaspoons mustard powder
1½ teaspoons ground turmeric
2 cups packed light brown sugar

MAKES ABOUT 3 LB

During the green bean growing season, I always become very popular; I do not grow my own beans, but most of the people living nearby do, as do many of my country friends, and they all seem to have far more beans than they know what to do with. I never look a gift horse in the mouth, and this recipe is what I do with the surplus. It is a lovely preserve to serve with cold meats for lunch or a light dinner, as part of a full meal, or spooned into a small bowl to eat with sandwiches.

1 Put the onions and ⅔ cup vinegar in a nonreactive pan and simmer gently for 10 to 15 minutes until the onions are tender.

2 Meanwhile, cook the beans in boiling salted water for five minutes. Drain the beans and add to the cooked onions.

3 Put the cornstarch, mustard powder, and turmeric in a small bowl and stir in enough of the remaining vinegar to make a smooth paste. Stir

the paste into the onion and bean mix and add the remaining vinegar. Simmer for 10 minutes.

4 Add the sugar and stir until it has dissolved. Then, simmer for another 15 minutes.

5 Divide the vegetables and liquid among warm, sterilized jars. Swirl the jars to disperse any air bubbles. Seal and leave to cool. Label the jars and store in a cool, dark, dry place for at least one month before eating.

Opposite: Mediterranean chutney

Eggplant slices in oil

2 eggplants, cut into ½ inch slices
Kosher salt (see method)
Extra virgin olive oil (see method)
2 rosemary sprigs
4 thyme sprigs

MAKES 5 CUPS

To make an attractive pattern on the eggplant slices, cook them twice on each side, turning them ninety degrees as you place them on the grill pan so the second set of grill marks will be at right angles to the first.

1 Layer the eggplant slices in a colander, sprinkling each layer with salt. Stand the colander on a plate, put a weighted plate on top, and leave overnight.

2 Rinse the eggplant slices well, drain, and dry with paper towels. Spread on a clean towel and leave to air-dry completely.

3 Put the eggplant slices in a bowl, and drizzle each side with olive oil.

4 Heat a large, heavy, grill pan until the heat can be felt rising from it when you put your hand about 1 inch above it. In batches, lay the eggplant slices in the pan and cook until they have grill marks on them. Turn the slices over and cook the other side until tender and also scored with grill marks. You might have

to adjust the heat beneath the pan during cooking. If the slices are marked before they are tender, reduce the heat. If they are tender but not marked, increase it.

5 Spread the slices on a wire rack to cool completely.

6 Pour a ½-inch layer of oil in the bottom of the jars you will be using. Divide the eggplant among the jars, stacking the slices and adding the oil as you go, and insert one rosemary sprig and two thyme sprigs in each jar. Top off the jars with more oil and seal. Label and store in a cool, dark, dry place for one month before eating. Keeps for up to six months.

Mozzarella and eggplant in carrozza

4 slices bread
1 medium piece fresh mozzarella cheese, sliced
Approximately 8 slices Eggplant Slices in Oil
2 anchovy fillets, cut in half (optional)
Large pinch of oregano
2 large eggs, beaten
Salt and freshly ground black pepper to taste
A little oil from the Eggplant Slices in Oil, for frying

SERVES 2

If you are not fond of anchovies, or do not have any in the cupboard, there is no need to abandon this savory, quick snack – simply use chopped Oven-dried Tomatoes with Herbs (see page 133) and black olives instead.

1 Place two slices of bread on the work surface. Cover with mozzarella cheese, then eggplant slices. Place a piece of anchovy on top and sprinkle with a little oregano.

2 Top with the remaining slices of bread and pinch the edges together.

3 Season the beaten eggs with salt and pepper. Soak both sides of each sandwich in the egg mixture.

4 Heat a thin layer of the oil in a skillet until it just starts to smoke. Add the sandwiches and fry on both sides until the outside is lightly golden and the cheese is beginning to melt. Drain briefly and quickly on paper towels and serve immediately.

Opposite: Mozzarella and eggplant in carrozza

Oil-cured mushrooms

Scant 2 cups olive oil

1 small onion, finely chopped

½ small red pepper, cored, seeded, and finely chopped

2 garlic cloves, chopped

Scant 2 cups white wine vinegar

1¼ cups water

A few sprigs of fresh thyme

A few sprigs of fresh parsley

A few sprigs of fresh tarragon

3 bay leaves

5 coriander seeds, crushed

10 black peppercorns, crushed

2 lb mixed mushrooms

MAKES ABOUT 3½ PINTS

I am fortunate enough to live in an area where there are quite a few locations for finding wild mushrooms, such as the New Forest, where I know of several fruitful places to visit. So each year, I have plenty for preserving in oil. This same recipe can also be used with store-bought mushrooms, whether the more "exotic" types, such as shiitake and chanterelle, or ordinary button mushrooms. Remember, never pick wild mushrooms unless an expert tells you they are safe to eat.

1 Heat a little of the oil in a large saucepan and sauté the onion, red pepper, and garlic until tender but not brown. Pour in the vinegar and water. Add the fresh herbs, bay leaves, coriander seeds, and peppercorns. Bring to a boil and continue to boil, uncovered, for five minutes.

2 Put the mushrooms in a large, nonreactive bowl and pour the contents of the pan over the mushrooms. Put a plate on top to keep the mushrooms under the surface of the liquid and leave in a cool place for 12 hours; stir the mushrooms occasionally.

3 Strain the liquid from the bowl. Dry all the vegetables and flavorings with paper towels, then spread them out on several layers of paper towels to air-dry completely.

4 Using a slotted spoon, pack some vegetables and flavorings into sterilized, dry, wide-necked jars. Slowly pour in enough oil to cover the vegetables. Continue adding vegetables and oil until the jar is filled. Press down on the contents of the jar and swirl to expel air bubbles.

5 Seal tightly. Store in a cool, dark, dry place for at least one month before eating.

Chunky mushroom "ketchup"

If this recipe is made with wild, field mushrooms instead of cultivated ones, the end-product will have the consistency of a smooth sauce. Use extreme caution when picking wild mushrooms, and never eat them unless you know they are safe. Use this "ketchup" to flavor meat dishes, mushroom dishes, or cheese and egg dishes where its color would not cause a problem.

1 Put the mushrooms in a nonreactive bowl and stir in the salt. Cover the bowl and leave in a cool place for 36 to 48 hours, stirring and squashing the mushrooms occasionally.

2 Pour the mushrooms and liquid into a nonreactive pan. Add the remaining ingredients and bring to the boil.

3 Boil cultivated mushrooms until nearly all their liquid has vanished. Then, with an immersion blender, blend the mushrooms until you get a chunky puree. Alternatively, you can use a regular blender. Reheat the puree until hot and spoon into warm sterilized jars, seal, and cool. Leave in a cool, dark place for one month before using.

4 If using wild mushrooms, proceed from step two and bring a boil, then simmer for about two hours. Strain through a fine, nonreactive sieve, then pour the liquid back into the pan and bring to the boil again. Pour into warm, sterilized bottles, and seal. The levels of salt and vinegar are sufficiently high to act as a preservative for the ketchup, providing the bottles are tightly sealed; if preferred, the ketchup can be processed for ten minutes in a boiling-water canner (see page 16). Label the bottles when cool.

$3\frac{1}{2}$ lb large, open, flat-capped mushrooms, such as portobello, quite finely chopped

3 tablespoons kosher salt

1 heaping teaspoon black peppercorns, lightly crushed

1 teaspoon allspice berries, lightly crushed

1 teaspoon whole cloves

$\frac{1}{2}$ teaspoon freshly grated nutmeg

$\frac{1}{4}$ cup red wine vinegar

MAKES AROUND 3 CUPS, DEPENDING UPON THE MOISTURE CONTENT OF THE MUSHROOMS

Creamy chicken with oil-cured mushrooms

2 tablespoons oil from the Oil-cured Mushrooms (see 122)

3 garlic cloves, chopped

1½ lb boneless chicken breasts, cut into strips

¾ cup medium-sweet Madeira wine

1 lb Oil-cured Mushrooms (see page 122), drained

Scant 1½ cups reduced-fat sour cream or crème fraîche

5 tablespoons chopped fresh tarragon

Salt and freshly ground black pepper to taste

SERVES 4

This impressive dish is quick to make and is ideal for entertaining or as a treat for yourself. Serve with mashed potatoes or pasta.

1 Heat the oil in a large skillet, add the garlic, and sauté for two to three minutes. Add the chicken and cook, stirring frequently, for five to six minutes until the chicken is golden and the juices run clear.

2 Add the Madeira, simmer for three to four minutes, then add the mushrooms, sour cream, tarragon, and salt and pepper. Heat through for about three minutes until the mushrooms and sour cream are hot.

Pickled shallots

1 cup kosher salt

5 cups water

2 lb shallots, peeled, with the root end left intact

2½ cups white wine vinegar

1½ cups sherry vinegar

⅔ cups balsamic vinegar

2 dried red chiles

1 slim cinnamon stick

5 allspice berries, crushed

2 blades of mace

2 bay leaves

MAKES ABOUT 4⅓ CUPS

Because shallots have a more gentle taste than onions, and the vinegars used in this recipe are all far less harsh than brown malt vinegar, it makes for a sophisticated, milder version of the old-fashioned favorite of pickled onions.

1 Put the salt into a non-metallic bowl and stir in the water. When the salt has dissolved, add the shallots. Put a weighted plate on top of the shallots to keep them under the water. Leave in a cool place for two days, stirring occasionally.

2 About two hours before you intend to pickle the shallots, put the vinegars, chiles, cinnamon, allspice, mace, and bay leaves in a nonreactive pan and bring slowly to a boil. Simmer for one minute, then remove from the heat and leave until cool.

3 Pour the shallots into a colander and rinse under cold running water. Drain, and dry thoroughly with a clean cloth. Spread out on another dry, clean cloth and let air-dry completely.

4 Pack the shallots into sterilized jars. Strain the vinegar through a cheesecloth-lined sieve and pour into the jars to completely cover the shallots. Swirl the jars to expel any trapped air bubbles. Seal tightly and label the jars. Leave in a cool, dark, dry place for at least one month before eating. Store for up to one year.

Opposite: Creamy chicken with oil-cured mushrooms

Savory red onion confiture

Onion confitures and marmalades have become popular in recent years. (Confiture is French for jam or preserves). Usually they are sweet-and-sour dishes of slowly cooked onions designed to be served immediately. But this version can be kept on the shelf for serving with sausages and potatoes, roast beef, or pork.

1 Heat the oil in a large skillet and add the onions, star anise, and peppercorns. Sprinkle with the salt, cover, and cook over low heat, stirring occasionally, until soft but not browned; the salt will draw out the water from the onions.

2 Stir in the sugar and continue to cook for another 15 minutes, stirring occasionally.

3 Pour in the vinegars and bring to a boil. Simmer gently until almost all the liquid has evaporated, stirring occasionally.

4 Prepare and fill the jars (see page 11) and heat-process in a boiling-water canner (see page 14). Let cool, label, and store in a cool, dark, dry place for two weeks before eating. Keeps for up to six months.

¼ cup peanut oil

3 lb red onions, some thinly sliced, some chopped

2 star anise, crushed

8 black peppercorns, crushed

2 teaspoons kosher salt

1 packed cup light brown sugar, or 1 cup granulated sugar

¾ cup raspberry vinegar

¾ cup sherry vinegar

¼ cup red wine vinegar

½ teaspoon ground allspice

MAKES 1 QUART

Squash and pineapple jam

This makes a lovely golden jam with the texture of a lightly jellied puree.

4 cups large cubes winter squash, such as butternut or kabocha

5 cups cubed fresh pineapple

2 tablespoons fresh lime or lemon juice

3½ cups granulated sugar

Commercial pectin (follow manufacturer's instructions for quantity and method)

Pat of butter

MAKES ABOUT 1½ LB

1 Put the squash in a nonreactive pan, just cover with water, and simmer until the squash is tender, stirring occasionally to ensure even cooking. Finely mash the squash in the pan with a potato masher.

2 Add the pineapple and lime or lemon juice to the pan with the mashed squash and simmer until the pineapple is tender.

3 Over low heat, stir in the sugar and pectin until they have dissolved, then increase the heat and boil the jam until it has thickened. Add the butter to disperse the scum.

4 Remove the pan from the heat and let stand 10 minutes before pouring. Prepare and fill the jars (see page 11) and heat-process in a boiling-water canner (see page 14). Leave overnight to cool. Label the jars and store in a cool, dark, dry place for up to nine months. Keep in the refrigerator after opening.

Squash chutney

With its golden color, flecked throughout with red, this chutney really stands out from the crowd.

2 lb finely chopped winter squash, such as butternut or kabocha

4 tablespoons finely chopped fresh ginger

1½ tablespoons finely crushed allspice berries

Pinch of crushed red pepper

1 onion, chopped

1 tart cooking apple, such as Granny Smith, cored and chopped without peeling

2 red bell peppers, chopped

2½ cups white wine vinegar

½ cup plus 1 tablespoon sugar

1 cup chopped dried mango

MAKES ABOUT 2¼ LB

1 Put the squash, ginger, allspice, and crushed red pepper in a nonreactive pan, just cover with water, and simmer until the squash is tender. Mash in the pan with a potato masher to the consistency you desire.

2 Add the onion, apple, red pepper, and vinegar to the pan and simmer until tender.

3 Over low heat, stir in the sugar and mango and heat gently, stirring, until the sugar has dissolved, then bring to a boil and simmer, stirring as necessary, until the chutney is thick. The chutney is ready when no liquid appears in the channel that is left when the spoon is drawn across the bottom of the pan. It will thicken further upon standing.

4 Ladle the chutney into hot, sterilized jars, and seal (see page 14). Let cool, label, and store in a cool, dark, dry place for at least one month before eating. Keeps for up to one year.

Opposite: Squash chutney

Squash marmalade

3 large oranges
¼ cup water
8 cups large cubes edible pumpkin, or other winter squash such as butternut or kabocha
8 cups granulated sugar
Commercial pectin (follow manufacturer's instructions for quantity method)

MAKES ABOUT 6 LB

In mainland Europe, marmalades are made with many different fruits, as well as oranges. This used to be the case in Britain, but in the nineteenth century, marmalade started to be made exclusively from oranges, principally Seville oranges from Spain. Today, Britain imports just about all of Spain's Seville orange crop. This marmalade has a thicker texture than an all-citrus fruit marmalade and a milder, fresher orange taste.

1 Quarter the oranges lengthwise and cut into slices as thin or thick as you like.

2 Put the orange slices in a small, nonreactive saucepan, add the water, and simmer, covered, for about 15 to 20 minutes until the peel is soft.

3 Put the squash in a larger nonreactive pan, pour in the water from the oranges (reserving the orange slices), cover, and cook until the squash is tender. Finely mash the squash in the pan with a potato masher.

4 Over low heat, stir the sugar and pectin into the squash until they have dissolved. Add the reserved oranges and boil hard until the setting point is reached (see page 23).

5 Remove the pan from the heat and let stand for 10 minutes. Prepare and fill the jars (see page 11) and heat-process in a boiling-water canner (see page 14). Let cool, label the jars, and keep in a cool, dark, dry place for up to six months.

Squash marmalade and apple brown betty

2½ cups unseasoned breadcrumbs
⅓ cup unsalted butter, melted
6 to 8 tablespoons Squash Marmalade
1¼ lb tart cooking apples, peeled, cored, and thinly sliced
Demerara (raw) sugar, for sprinkling

SERVES 4

Brightly colored flashes of pumpkin marmalade among the apples adds an intriguing, fruity sweetness to the apple in this old-fashioned favorite.

1 Preheat the oven to 350°F. Toss the breadcrumbs with the butter until thoroughly coated. Press an even layer over the base of a medium shallow baking dish, reserving some for the top.

2 Stir the marmalade into the apples and pack the mixture into the dish, making sure the top is level. Cover with the remaining breadcrumbs, patting them into place. Sprinkle demerara sugar over the top and bake for about 30 to 40 minutes until the apple is tender and the top is brown and crisp.

Opposite: Squash marmalade and apple brown betty

Spiced tomato chutney

Of all the recipes for chutney, there must be more for tomato chutney than for any other, and over the years, I have tried many of them. This is my favorite, at least for the time being; tastes change, or I may come across a new version that I'd prefer to this one.

1 Put all the ingredients in a nonreactive pan, bring to a boil, and simmer, stirring as necessary, until the chutney is thick. The chutney is ready when no liquid appears in the channel that is left when the spoon is drawn across the bottom of the pan. It will thicken further upon standing.

2 Prepare and fill the jars (see page 11) and heat-process in a boiling-water canner (see page 14). Let cool, label the jars and store in a cool, dark, dry place for one month before eating. Keep for up to one year.

2 large red onions, chopped

4 to 6 large garlic cloves, chopped

1 red bell pepper, chopped

1/2 lb tart cooking apples, cored and chopped without peeling

1 fresh red chile pepper, seeded if preferred, finely chopped

6 tablespoons finely chopped fresh ginger

3 tablespoons ground cumin

2 tablespoons dried oregano

2 1/4 lb firm but ripe tomatoes, cored and chopped

1 cup red wine vinegar

1/2 cup firmly packed light brown sugar, or granulated sugar

MAKES ABOUT 2 1/2 LB

Oven-dried tomatoes with herbs

A few years ago, I felt it was not worth drying tomatoes at home, due to the poor taste of the many tomato varieties that were available. But now that the flavor and succulence of tomatoes have improved dramatically, I think making your own dried tomatoes and packing them in oil is one of the best ways of preserving them.

1 Preheat the oven to its lowest setting. Line the bottom of the oven with foil to protect it from drips.

2 Halve the tomatoes lengthwise, and scoop out the seeds using a teaspoon. As each half is ready, place it cut-side down on a few layers of paper towels.

3 Sprinkle salt very lightly on each piece of tomato and place, cut-side down, on a wire rack, spaced slightly apart. Put the racks in the oven and prop the door slightly ajar. This is done so the tomatoes dry out rather than cook.

4 Leave the tomatoes for six to 12 hours, depending on the size of the tomatoes and the temperature of the oven, until they feel dry to the touch but are still slightly fleshy; they should not become papery. Remove from the oven and let cool.

5 Loosely pack the tomatoes in sterilized, dry jars, adding the herbs as you go. Pour in oil to cover the tomatoes by 1/2 inch. Swirl the jar to expel any air bubbles and seal. Label the jar and store in a cool, dark, dry place for at least two to four weeks before eating. Keeps for up to six months.

6 lb fleshy, ripe tomatoes (the fleshier and more flavorful, the better)

Sea salt (see method)

Several sprigs of fresh rosemary, plus a combination of other fresh herbs, such as basil, thyme, marjoram, or oregano

1 bay leaf

About 2 1/2 cups virgin olive oil

MAKES ABOUT 4 1/3 CUPS

Opposite: Spiced tomato chutney

Roasted tomato sauce

3 lb ripe plum tomatoes, halved
4 garlic cloves
5 thyme sprigs
1 rosemary sprig
Salt and black pepper to taste
2 teaspoons superfine sugar
Olive oil, for drizzling

MAKES ABOUT 2½ CUPS

Roasting the tomatoes concentrates their flavor, making a wonderfully rich-tasting sauce. To give the sauce a Mediterranean flavor, chopped black olives, anchovy fillets, and fresh herbs can be added after pureeing.

1 Preheat the oven to 425°F. Pack the tomatoes, cut side up, in a single layer in lightly oiled roasting pan. Scatter the garlic and herbs over the tomatoes. Sprinkle with salt, pepper, the sugar, and drizzle with a little olive oil. Roast the tomatoes for about 20 minutes until the edges have blackened. Lower the oven temperature to 350°F and continue to roast the tomatoes for 45 to 50 minutes until the tomatoes have shrunk in size.

2 Discard the herb sprigs and puree the tomatoes with the garlic. For a really smooth sauce, press through a nonreactive fine sieve.

3 Let the sauce cool, then pour into a freezer-proof, heavy-duty container to within 1 inch of the top, to allow for expansion. Freeze until solid. Cover with a rigid lid, or with heavy-duty polythene, and seal it tightly. Label with the contents and date of packing.

4 Chill the sauce, then place in the freezer. When frozen, cover the container and store for up to three months.

5 To use the sauce, thaw in the refrigerator overnight, or at room temperature for about four hours.

Tomato ketchup

3 lb ripe tomatoes, chopped
2 red onions, chopped
2 celery stalks, chopped
2 garlic cloves, crushed (optional)
1 cup firmly packed light brown sugar, or granulated sugar
⅔ cup cider vinegar
½ teaspoon cayenne pepper
1½ teaspoons paprika
2 teaspoons sun-dried tomato paste (optional)
½ teaspoon kosher salt

MAKES ABOUT 2½ CUPS

This is so different from the sweet, but otherwise bland, commercial tomato ketchup that you might have difficulty persuading people that it really is ketchup. If the tomatoes you are using are not very ripe and flavorful, boost their taste by adding about 2 teaspoons sun-dried tomato paste.

1 Put the tomatoes, onions, celery, and garlic if using, into a nonreactive pan and cook over a very low heat until the tomatoes become pulpy. Increase the heat and boil until the mixture thickens, stirring frequently.

2 Press through a nonreactive fine sieve and return to the rinsed pan. Over low heat, stir in the remaining ingredients until the sugar has dissolved, then simmer until the mixture thickens, stirring as necessary.

3 Prepare and fill screw-top bottles (see page 11), and heat-process in a boiling-water canner (see page 16).

4 Transfer the bottles from the boiling-water canner to a wooden board and let cool. Label and store in a cool, dark, dry place for at least one month before using. Keeps for up to one year.

Opposite: Roasted tomato sauce

Dried tomato and chive drop scones

1 cup cottage cheese, drained

2 large eggs, separated

$2/3$ cup self-rising flour

6 halves Oven-dried Tomatoes with Herbs (see page 133), chopped

3 tablespoons chopped chives

Salt and freshly ground black pepper to taste

About 3 tablespoons milk

Olive oil for cooking

SERVES 4

Small, airy, cottage cheese drop scones, flavored with dried tomatoes and chives, makes for an appetizing dish to be served for breakfast or brunch. They can, of course, be served at other times of the day, such as for a light lunch, as an appetizer, or a snack. Keep in mind that the amount of milk you will need depends upon the moistness of the cottage cheese.

1 Beat together the cottage cheese, and egg yolks, then stir in the flour. Whisk the egg whites until stiff but not dry. Stir a tablespoonful of the whipped egg whites into the mixture, then gently fold in the remaining egg whites in two batches, adding the dried tomatoes, chives, and salt and pepper towards the end of the second batch. Add enough milk to make a mixture that falls off the spoon when given a light shake.

2 Heat a little oil in a large nonstick skillet. Add large tablespoonfuls of the mixture to the pan, and spread them lightly with the back of the spoon. Cook for two to three minutes until browned underneath, then carefully turn them over and brown the other side.

Zucchini chutney

$1\frac{1}{2}$ lb zucchini, coarsely chopped or thickly sliced

Kosher salt for sprinkling

2 onions, chopped

3 garlic cloves, chopped

1 cup raisins

$1/2$ tablespoon black peppercorns, crushed

2 tablespoons chopped fresh ginger

$1\frac{1}{2}$ teaspoons celery salt

$3\frac{1}{4}$ cups white wine vinegar

$1\frac{2}{3}$ cups light brown sugar

MAKES ABOUT 2 LB

For the best flavor, use small zucchini. Once they grow large, they become more watery, and therefore more flavor is lost during the salting.

1 Layer the zucchini in a colander, sprinkling the layers with salt. Place on a plate and leave overnight to drain.

2 The next day, rinse the zucchini under cold running water, drain, and pat dry with a clean cloth. Put the zucchini into a nonreactive pan with the onion, garlic, raisins, peppercorns, ginger, celery salt, and vinegar. Bring to a boil, and boil gently for about 15 minutes until the onions and zucchini are tender.

3 Stir in the sugar until it has dissolved, then simmer steadily until the mixture is thick; stir frequently to prevent sticking. The chutney is ready when no liquid appears in the channel that is left when the spoon is drawn across the bottom of the pan. It will thicken further upon standing.

4 Prepare and fill the jars (see page 11), and heat-process in a boiling-water canner (see page 14). Let cool, label the jars and store in a cool, dark, dry place for at least one month before eating. Keeps for one year.

Zucchini chutney

Italian vegetable pickle

When neatly packed, these jars of pickles look so satisfyingly impressive on the pantry or cupboard shelf that it makes the trouble and care taken seem worthwhile. But their attractiveness is their downfall, because all too soon someone won't be able to resist temptation and will delve indiscriminately into a jar to try some of its contents (why is it nearly always from the bottom) and the whole effect will be ruined.

1 Layer the vegetables except the garlic in a large, non-metallic bowl, sprinkling salt between the layers. Pour the water over the vegetables. Put a weighted plate on top to keep the vegetables under the water. Leave in a cool place overnight.

2 The next day, pour the vegetables into a colander and rinse under cold running water. Drain, and dry thoroughly with a clean cloth. Spread out on another dry, clean cloth and let air-dry completely.

3 Transfer the vegetables to a bowl and mix in the garlic and oils.

4 Pour a thin layer of vinegar into hot, sterilized jars. Divide half the chiles and herbs among the jars. Pack in the vegetables as tightly as possible. When the jars are about half-filled, add the remaining chiles and herbs. Continue filling the jars.

5 Pour in enough vinegar to cover the vegetables and come to within $\frac{1}{4}$-inch of the top of the jars, pressing the vegetables down. Swirl the jars to expel air bubbles and seal. Let cool, then label and store in a cool, dark, dry place for at least one month before eating. Keeps for up to six months in a cool, dark, dry place.

$\frac{1}{2}$ lb zucchini, cut into matchstick strips
$\frac{1}{2}$ lb trimmed fennel, cut into matchstick strips
$\frac{3}{4}$ lb eggplant, cut into matchstick strips
1 lb red onions, cut through the root into 8 wedges
1 red bell pepper, cut into strips
1 yellow bell pepper, cut into strips
2 celery sticks, sliced
$\frac{1}{3}$ lb baby radishes
$\frac{1}{4}$ lb button mushrooms, stalks trimmed
$\frac{3}{4}$ cup kosher salt
$7\frac{1}{2}$ cups water
5 garlic cloves, cut into slivers
4 tablespoons extra virgin olive oil
3 tablespoons walnut oil
$6\frac{1}{4}$ to $8\frac{3}{4}$ cups white wine vinegar
4 dried chile peppers
8 small sprigs each of fresh thyme and fresh rosemary
8 small bay leaves

MAKES ABOUT $8\frac{2}{3}$ CUPS

Zucchini chutney and cheese loaf

1¼ cups self-rising flour

1¼ cups self-rising, whole wheat flour

Salt and freshly ground black pepper to taste

1½ teaspoons baking powder

1 stick unsalted butter, diced

Scant 1 cup milk

Handful of parsley, coarsely chopped

6 tablespoons Zucchini Chutney (see page 136)

½ lb fontina, fresh mozzarella, Gruyère, or cheddar cheese, grated

1 large red onion, very finely chopped

SERVES 4 TO 6

I like to use a cheese that melts well, such as fontina or, failing that, fresh mozzarella or aged Gruyere, especially if the bread is served while still warm, when it is at its best. If the bread is going to be served cold, I use a fairly mature cheddar cheese instead (immature cheeses are less appetizing because they have little taste and become more oily during cooking). Other chutneys that can be used in this recipe are Spiced Tomato Chutney (see page 133), Red Pepper Chutney (see page 112), and Mediterranean Chutney (see page 118).

1 Preheat the oven to 400°F. Sift the flours, salt and pepper, and baking powder into a bowl. Add the butter and, using a pastry blender, cut it in until the mixture resembles breadcrumbs.

2 Stir in the milk and parsley to make a soft dough. If too dry, add a little more milk.

3 Turn the dough out onto a lightly floured surface and divide it in half. Roll one half to a square, rectangle, or circle about ½- to ¾-inch thick and put on a baking sheet. Spread the chutney over the dough, leaving a ½-inch border around the edges. Sprinkle with all but 2 tablespoons of the cheese and the onion. Season with black pepper, and brush the border with water.

4 Roll out the remaining dough to fit over the first piece, position it in place, and press the edges together lightly to seal them. Sprinkle with the remaining cheese.

5 Bake on the top rack of the oven for 10 minutes, then transfer it to the middle rack and bake for 30 minutes or until crisp and brown.

6 Transfer to a wire rack to cool for 10 minutes before serving.

Tarragon and orange jelly

4 lb oranges, halved and sliced
   into semi-circles
1 lb lemons, halved and sliced
   into semi-circles
12½ cups water
Granulated sugar or preserving
   sugar (see method)
2 tablespoons tarragon leaves

MAKES ABOUT 5½ LB

Golden, fragrant herb jellies like this one are ideal for serving with roast and grilled meats, poultry, and game – either spooned on the plate, or stirred into the cooking juices to make a light sauce. Herb jellies are also good with pâtés, and this one goes well with fish like salmon and trout. Other herbs, such as thyme or mint, can be used instead of tarragon.

1 Put the oranges and lemons in a nonreactive pan with the water. Bring to a boil, then simmer gently for about 1½ hours until the fruit is soft.

2 Pour the contents of the pan into a jelly bag suspended over a nonreactive bowl and leave overnight in a cool place to drip.

3 Discard the pulp in the jelly bag. Measure the juice and pour into a clean pan. Add 2¼ cups sugar for each 2½ cups juice. Add the tarragon. Heat

gently, stirring, until the sugar has dissolved, then boil hard for about 15 minutes until the setting point is reached (see page 23).

4 Remove any scum with a slotted spoon and let the jelly stand for 15 minutes. Stir to distribute the tarragon. Prepare and fill the jars (see page 11), and heat-process in a boiling-water canner(see page 14). Leave overnight. Label the cool jars and store in a cool, dark, dry place for up to one year.

Crystallized flowers

If you grow flowers throughout the year, you will always have an appropriate seasonal decoration to use for desserts and cakes. Your choice of flowers must be governed by one principle – they must be edible. Only use flowers or blossoms that you are positive are safe for human consumption. In addition, never use flowers or leaves that have been sprayed with pesticides or fertilizer. Stay away from flowers that are purchased from a florist, and never use flowers that have been picked from the side of the road. Try to choose blossoms that are richly perfumed, such as roses, violets, and mock orange blossom. Gum arabic is available from specialty stores, but if you can't find it, egg white can be used instead, although the decorated flowers will not keep as long.

Gum arabic, or egg white (see note)
Few drops of rose water or orange flower water, if using gum arabic; pinch of salt, if using egg white (see method)
Edible flowers (see method)
Superfine sugar (see method)

1 Divide large flowers, such as roses, into petals, leaving a short piece of stalk on each one if possible.

2 If using gum arabic, mix it with the flower water following the packet instructions until completely dissolved; as a general guide, use 1 tablespoon gum arabic to 2 tablespoons flower water. If using egg white, beat it with the salt until frothy.

3 Using a small, fine artist's paintbrush, carefully paint the gum arabic or egg white evenly over the flowers, inside and out, making sure they are completely covered.

4 Sprinkle the flowers with an even, generous layer of superfine sugar. Shake off any excess. Carefully put on a wire rack and leave to dry.

5 If necessary, sprinkle with a second layer of sugar to make sure the petals are evenly coated. Leave in a warm, well-ventilated place to dry completely; they should be hard and dry to the touch. Store in an airtight container or jar between layers of waxed paper. They will keep for up to one year.

NOTE Do not use foxgloves, anything from the solanum family (which includes potatoes and tomatoes, as well as the climbing garden plant), delphiniums, sweet peas, or flowers from any bulbs including hyacinths and lilies. If you do not know for certain that a flower is safe to eat, do not use it without checking its safety.

Rose petal jam

Select roses that are just coming into full bloom, and have not been sprayed with fertilizers or pesticides, or grown near a busy road. Pick the roses in the morning when any dew has disappeared and before the sun becomes too hot.

1 Separate the petals from the roses. Rinse the petals carefully and gently pat them dry with a clean cloth. Tear out the white "heel" from the petals, then tear them into small pieces, being careful not to make them too small.

2 Put the petals, sugar, and pectin in a bowl and stir. Cover and leave for about 24 hours.

3 Pour the water into a nonreactive pan. Add the lemon juice and heat gently, stirring, until the sugar has dissolved. Add the contents of the bowl with the petals and sugar, cover, raise the heat slightly, and simmer for 20 minutes.

4 Increase the heat further, and boil the jam until it is just about at the setting point. Add the rose water if the jam lacks flavor, and food coloring if it is too pale.

5 Let the jam stand for 10 minutes, then stir to distribute the petals, and ladle into warm, sterilized jars. Seal (page 11) and leave overnight to cool. Label the jars and store in a cool, dark, dry place for up to six months.

About 8 oz very fragrant, dark red roses, 10 to 12 heads (see recipe note)

2 cups granulated sugar

Commercial pectin (follow manufacturer's instructions for quantity and method)

3 cups plus 2 tablespoons water

Juice of 2 lemons

Rose water, to taste (optional)

Food coloring (optional)

MAKES ABOUT 2 LB

Trout and pickled ginger salad

Japanese pickled ginger

Traditionally, pickled ginger is served with sushi and sashimi, but it goes equally well with other seafood, especially shellfish, grilled salmon and trout, and even poultry. It can also be finely diced and added to salads, or simply nibbled as a palate cleanser. The pickled ginger will naturally be a yellowish or pale salmon color, or it may be dyed various shades of pink, from subtle to garish, with the addition of fresh red plum juice or a few drops of red food coloring. In Japan, very young ginger is used for this dish, but as it is extremely difficult to buy in the United States, use ginger that has a good sheen and is not fibrous.

½ lb fresh ginger
Sea salt (see method)
1¼ cups rice vinegar
1 tablespoon superfine sugar
A few drops red food coloring

MAKES ABOUT 1½ CUPS

1 Peel the ginger and cut into wafer thin slices following the line of the grain. Steep the slices in cold water for 30 minutes, then drain.

2 Add the ginger to a pan of boiling water, return quickly to a boil, and drain again. Leave to cool. Pack into a sterilized jar, sprinkling with salt as you go.

3 Gently heat the vinegar and sugar, stirring until the sugar has dissolved. Add the red food coloring, if using, and pour over the ginger to cover it completely. Seal and leave in a cool place for two weeks, shaking the jar occasionally until the salt has dissolved.

4 Transfer to the refrigerator. Use within three months.

Trout and pickled ginger salad

The clean, fresh taste of pickled ginger sprinkled over poached trout or salmon will give the fish a great flavor boost. If you have some fish stock, it can be used instead of water for poaching the trout.

2 trout, each weighing about ¾ lb, at room temperature
Boiling water (for poaching the trout)
5 tablespoons peanut or vegetable oil
1 tablespoon lime juice
Salt and freshly ground black pepper to taste
3 handfuls of crisp lettuce leaves, torn into bite-sized pieces
1 handful of baby spinach leaves
4 teaspoons finely chopped Japanese Pickled Ginger
Chopped cilantro, for garnish

SERVES 4 AS A FIRST COURSE

1 Lay the trout in a large frying pan that just fits the fish. Cover the fish with boiling water and heat until bubbles begin to appear in the water. Cover and maintain this temperature for about 12 minutes, until the trout is cooked through.

2 Using a spatula, lift the trout from the pan. Remove the skin, if desired. Carefully lift the trout fillets from the bone and set aside. You will now have four fillets.

3 Whisk together the peanut oil, lime juice, salt, and pepper to make a dressing. Toss together the lettuce and spinach, pour the dressing over the greens, and toss again. Divide among four plates, garnish with the cilantro, and top with a trout fillet. Sprinkle the ginger over the fish. Serve.

4 The salad can be varied by flaking the fish and stirring it into the salad, before sprinkling with ginger strips. See photograph.

Pickled walnuts

1 lb green walnuts
1 cup salt
5 cups water
$1\frac{1}{2}$ oz fresh ginger
$7\frac{1}{2}$ cups white wine vinegar
3 oz black peppercorns
$1\frac{1}{2}$ oz allspice berries, lightly crushed

MAKES ABOUT $8\frac{3}{4}$ CUPS

Pickled walnuts have always been considered one of the essential country preserves. Green walnuts are not for sale in the US, but it is worth finding someone who has a walnut tree. The nuts must be harvested when the outer skin (which becomes the hard, brown shell) is still soft and green without any signs of hardening; this is usually at the end of summer. It is a good idea to wear rubber gloves or similar hand covering when picking and handling the nuts otherwise your hands will become stained by a color that is very difficult to remove.

1 Prick the walnuts well all over with a darning needle and put them in a nonreactive bowl.

2 Dissolve $\frac{1}{2}$ cup of the salt in $2\frac{1}{2}$ cups of the water, pour over the nuts, and cover. Leave for one week to remove excess bitterness.

3 Drain off and throw away the liquid. Dissolve the remaining salt in the remaining water, pour over the nuts, and leave for two more weeks.

4 Drain the nuts (discarding the liquid), rinse, and dry. Spread the nuts out and leave exposed to the air for two to three weeks until they have turned black.

5 Pack the nuts into clean, dry jars.

6 Bruise the ginger with the flat of a knife, then put in a nonreactive pan with the vinegar, peppercorns and allspice berries. Boil for 10 minutes before pouring over the nuts. Swirl the jar to expel any air bubbles.

7 Seal and let cool. Store in a cool, dark, dry place for at least one month before eating. Keep for one to two years.

Chestnuts in syrup

About $1\frac{1}{2}$ lb fresh chestnuts in their shells
1 whole vanilla bean
1 cup plus 2 tablespoons sugar
1 cup liquid glucose
$\frac{3}{4}$ cup water
2 tablespoons dark rum or brandy

MAKES ABOUT $1\frac{1}{2}$ LB

These sweet mouthfuls are prepared in a way that is similar to candying, so keep in mind that this recipe takes several days to complete, although there is very little to do on each day and the results are well worth the time and minimal effort. Have a few extra chestnuts just in case any are bad.

1 Cut a slit in the skin of each chestnut and add to a pan of boiling water. Simmer for 10 minutes then remove from the heat. Using a slotted spoon, scoop out the nuts one at a time. When just cool enough to handle, peel off both the outer skin and the thin inner skin.

2 Simmer the nuts with the vanilla bean in just enough water to cover until the nuts are just tender but not breaking up. Drain and dry with paper towels; reserve the vanilla bean.

3 In a pan large enough to hold the nuts, gently heat the sugar and liquid glucose in $\frac{3}{4}$ cup water, stirring, until

the sugar has dissolved. Increase the heat until the syrup is boiling, then remove the pan from the heat and add the nuts. Return to the heat and bring back to a boil. Take the pan from the heat, cover, and leave overnight.

4 The next day, remove the lid and return the pan to a boil. Take off the heat again, cover once more, and leave for another night. The following morning, return the vanilla bean to the pan and bring to a boil, uncovered, for the last time. Off the heat, add the rum or brandy and pour the chestnuts, vanilla bean, and syrup into a prepared jar (see page 11). Swirl the jar to ensure no air bubbles are trapped and seal. Heat-process in a boiling-water canner (see page 16). Let cool and label. Store in a cool, dark, dry place for one month before eating. Use within one year.

Chestnut and vanilla jam

This luscious jam is very easy to make once the chestnuts have been peeled, and because there is no need to worry about getting the setting point right; the mixture just has to be boiled until it is thick.

About 2¾ lb fresh chestnuts in their shells
1 whole vanilla bean
3½ cups light brown sugar
2 tablespoons dark rum

MAKES ABOUT 3 LB

1 Cut a slit in the skin of each chestnut and add to a pan of boiling water. Simmer for 10 minutes then remove from the heat. Using a slotted spoon, scoop out the nuts one at a time. When just cool enough to handle, peel off both the outer skin and the thin inner skin.

2 Simmer the nuts with the vanilla bean in just enough water to cover until the nuts are very tender. Drain the nuts, reserving the water and the vanilla bean. Puree the nuts. Weigh the puree; there should be about lb 10oz.

3 Put the puree, sugar, and a scant ½ cup of the reserved cooking water into a heavy pan. Split the reserved vanilla bean, scrape out the seeds, and add the seeds and the pod to the pan. Heat gently, stirring, until the sugar has dissolved, then bring to a boil. Boil until thick, stirring frequently. Add the rum and discard the vanilla pod.

4 Prepare and fill the jars (see page 11), and heat-process in a boiling water canner (see page 14). Leave overnight to cool and set slightly. Label the jars and store in a cool, dry place for up to six months.

Thai-flavored gravlax

2 tablespoons kosher salt

2 tablespoons superfine sugar

2½-lb wild salmon, center-cut, filleted but not skinned

2 lemon grass stalks, lower part, outer leaves removed, very finely chopped

Grated rind of 2 limes

1½ teaspoons coriander seeds, dry-roasted and crushed

2-inch piece fresh ginger, grated

Freshly ground black pepper to taste

5 tablespoons finely chopped cilantro

3 tablespoons finely chopped fresh mint

SERVES 8-10

For an easy first course that can be made in advance and sits happily in the fridge until you want it, this recipe couldn't be better. I serve the gravlax on a bed of crisp lettuce leaves and cilantro, along with mayonnaise that has been flavored with lime juice. To make canapés, I put a dab of the above-mentioned mayonnaise on small pieces of crisp toast, then loosely "drape" thin slices of the gravlax and very thin slices of cucumber on top, and finally garnish with cilantro. I prefer using wild salmon, which has a firmer, leaner flesh and provides a better flavor than farmed fish.

1 Mix the salt and sugar together and rub well into both sides of the salmon. Combine the remaining ingredients and rub these into the salmon.

2 Lay the fish skin-side up in a shallow dish or small tray and wrap tightly in plastic wrap. Weigh down with weights or cans.

3 Leave in the bottom of the refrigerator for three days, turning the fish over daily and spooning any juices back over the fish.

4 To serve the gravlax, remove the plastic wrap, wipe off the excess marinade, and cut the fish into thin slices using a long, sharp, narrow-bladed knife held almost parallel to the fish.

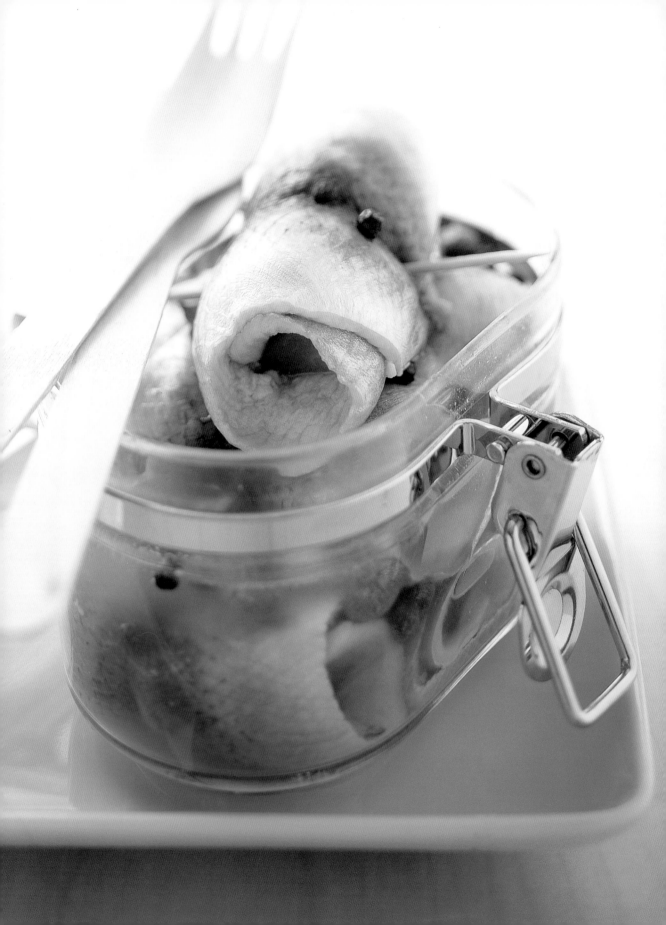

Potted shrimp with Mediterranean herbs

For best results, use small shrimp that have just been cooked. Pair with warm ciabatta bread for an appetizer, or a crisp salad for a light lunch. Also try the shrimp stirred into a risotto or tossed with pasta.

1 Gently melt 1 stick plus 2 tablespoons of the butter. Toss the shrimp with the herbs and salt and pepper. Gently stir the shrimp into the melted butter, cover, and heat very gently for 5 to 10 minutes so the shrimp become impregnated with the butter.

2 Pack the mixture into six sterilized, individual soufflé dishes or ramekins, making sure there are no air pockets. Leave until cool.

3 Gently heat the remaining butter until it starts to foam, then remove from the heat and let stand for a few minutes until the milky sediment falls to the bottom of the pan. Carefully pour the clear liquid butter over the shrimp to make a top layer that covers the shrimp. Discard the milky sediment left in the pan.

4 Let the pots cool, then cover and refrigerate for one day before eating. Serve within one week. Once the butter seal has been broken, eat within a day.

2 sticks unsalted butter, diced

1 lb peeled, freshly cooked small shrimp, a few chopped coarsely

2 to 3 tablespoons chopped fresh basil

2 to 3 tablespoons chopped mixed fresh herbs, such as thyme, tarragon, oregano, chives, and rosemary

Salt and freshly ground black pepper to taste

SERVES 6

Rollmop herrings

Serve as an appetizer accompanied by light brown bread, as part of a buffet, or with a crisp green salad or potato salad as a light lunch.

1 Put the salt and 4½ cups water in a nonreactive saucepan and bring to a boil; stir occasionally to make sure the salt dissolves. Let cool.

2 Put the herrings in a large, nonreactive dish. Pour the brine over them, making sure the fish is completely covered. Cover and refrigerate for 24 hours.

3 Meanwhile, add the vinegar, 2¼ cups water, juniper berries, mace, and allspice berries into a saucepan. Bring to a boil. Simmer for 10 minutes, then let cool.

4 Remove the herrings from the brine, rinse thoroughly, and lay them flat on a board, skin-side down.

5 Divide the gherkins among the herrings. Roll each herring from head to tail, and secure with a toothpick.

6 Pack the rollmops into cold, sterilized jars and divide the onion, bay leaves, peppercorns, and capers among them. Strain in the spiced vinegar to within ¼ inch of the top and seal. Refrigerate for at least four days before eating. The rollmops will keep for several weeks.

1 cup salt

4½ cups water

Eight ½-lb herrings, cleaned, and boned through the backbone

2¼ cups white wine vinegar

2¼ cups water

2 teaspoons juniper berries, crushed

1 blade of mace (optional)

1 teaspoon allspice berries, crushed

4 large gherkin pickles, cut into thick spears as long as the width of the herrings

1 onion, thinly sliced into rings

2 to 3 bay leaves

12 black peppercorns

2 tablespoons capers

MAKES 8

Opposite: Rollmop herrings

Rillettes

¼ lb fresh pork back fat, chopped

2 lb fresh blade bone or belly of pork, plus some bones

1 shallot, chopped

2 sprigs of fresh thyme

3 sprigs fresh parsley

1 bay leaf

Pinch of *quatre épices* (a French spice blend) or mixed spice

Salt and freshly ground black pepper to taste

5 tablespoons water

SERVES 6

Delicious, rich rillettes (shredded, potted pork) are made throughout France, but they are a particular speciality of the Loire region. I have tasted many during the time I have spent in the area, and each cook has his or her special touch that makes their rillettes unique (and according to the cook, the best). Rillettes are very easy to make at home, providing the right pork is used – it must be fresh, not frozen. *Quatre épices* is a French spice blend, available from gourmet or specialty stores. Sealed tightly with fat, the rillettes may be kept in the fridge for a snack, as a first course, or for a light lunch. The rillettes I make do not have as high a fat content as many found in France.

1 Preheat the oven to 275°F. Put the fat back into a heavy pot and place in the oven to melt.

2 Cut the pork into small pieces and add to the melted fat along with the shallot, bones, thyme, parsley, bay leaf, *quatre épices*, salt and pepper, and water. Leave to cook very slowly (the fat must not bubble) in the oven for about four hours, stirring occasionally, until the meat is almost falling apart. Add more water if the pot appears to get too dry.

3 Discard the bones and herbs from the pot. Strain the meat through a sieve placed over a bowl to catch the fat and juices; reserve these.

4 Using a fork, tear the meat into shreds, then pack into small, sterilized earthenware pots to come to within $\frac{1}{2}$-inch of the top.

5 Remove the reserved fat, which will have separated from the reserved juices, heat it, and pour over the rillettes to fill the pots and seal out the air. Leave to cool, then store in the refrigerator for at least one day. Return to room temperature for at least 30 minutes before eating. Eat within four to five days

Hot-smoked pork chops with ginger, lime, and cilantro

The long, slow hot-smoking process keeps the chops moist and impregnates them with a delicious flavor, which is best appreciated if they are served with simple accompaniments, such as mashed potatoes and a salad, or grilled tomatoes and mushrooms.

1 Place the chops in a single layer in a nonreactive dish. Mix together the remaining ingredients except the cilantro. Pour the marinade over the chops, then turn them over. Cover and leave in a cool place for four hours, turning the chops over occasionally.

2 Assemble and prepare the smoker according to the manufacturer's instructions.

3 Lift the chops from the marinade; reserve the marinade. Put the chops on the smoker's cooking rack, cover, and smoke at 200 to 250°F for two to three hours until the internal temperature of the chops reaches 160°F. Brush with the reserved marinade two or three times during smoking.

4 Transfer the chops to warmed serving plates, sprinkle with salt and the chopped cilantro, and serve.

4 pork chops
1 tablespoon finely chopped fresh ginger
1 small garlic clove, finely chopped
2 tablespoons soy sauce
1$\frac{1}{2}$ tablespoons sesame oil
4 tablespoons peanut or vegetable oil
Juice of 2 limes
Kosher salt and freshly ground black pepper to taste
3 tablespoons chopped cilantro

SERVES 4

Country pork pâté

Traditionally, a pork pâté would contain both a fatty cut of pork, such as belly of pork, and extra pork fat – not only to assist with the keeping qualities, but to prevent the cooked pâté from being dry. In this recipe, I have tried to compromise between the need for succulence in the pâté and modern preference for less fat. Variations on the recipe include flavoring it with strips of chorizo or salami, and substituting cooked mushrooms for the olives. To make a pâté that has a firm texture for slicing without having to press it, add 1½ cups breadcrumbs; this also retains the juices within the pâté rather than pressing them to the outside.

1 Preheat the oven to 325°F. Heat the butter in a skillet, add the onion and garlic and sauté until soft. Set aside to cool.

2 Grind the pork, veal, liver, and prosciutto or pancetta together. Then, using your hands, mix with the remaining ingredients except the bacon slices until thoroughly combined. Break off a small piece of the mixture and sauté it in order to taste and check the seasoning.

3 Line a 5-cup terrine with bacon slices, leaving the ends overhanging the sides.

4 Pack layers of the meat mixture into the terrine, making sure there are no air pockets. Fold the bacon over the pâté to cover it. Put the lid on the mould, or cover it with a double thickness of foil.

5 Put the terrine in a roasting pan, place the pan on the oven rack, and pour boiling water around to come halfway up the sides. Cook for about two hours until the sides have shrunk slightly from the terrine and a skewer inserted in the center and left there for 30 seconds then touched to the back of the hand feels warm; the internal temperature should be 170°F.

6 Remove the terrine mold from the water and let cool for about one hour. Uncover the mold and weight the top with a 2 lb weight or filled cans. Leave to cool completely. Refrigerate, still weighted, for one to two days before serving.

7 Return the pâté to room temperature for 30 minutes before serving, either from the mold, or inverted onto a serving plate or board and cut into ½ inch slices. The pâté will keep for two to three days in the refrigerator. It can also be frozen for up to one month either: in the terrine; unmolded whole and wrapped first in plastic wrap, then in heavy-duty foil; or cut into slices and each slice wrapped individually in plastic wrap, then heavy-duty foil. To thaw, loosen the wrapping and leave in the refrigerator overnight.

2 tablespoons butter

1 large onion, finely chopped

3 to 4 garlic cloves, finely chopped

1 lb uncured pork belly (check with your local butcher for this rare cut), or pork fatback

About ⅓ lb veal

About ⅓ lb chicken livers

Scant ⅓ lb piece prosciutto or pancetta, chopped

½ cup pitted black olives, chopped

5 tablespoons chopped mixed herbs such as thyme, oregano, parsley, basil, tarragon and rosemary

2 to 3 tablespoons brandy

Salt and freshly ground black pepper to taste

About 8 bacon slices

SERVES 6 TO 8

Pickled eggs

At one time, a king-sized jar of these savory hard-boiled eggs could be found on the bar of many pubs throughout Britain. Pickled eggs make an interesting addition to salads and sandwiches, picnics, or served as part of an antipasto or mezze spread. They are very simple to make and it is well worth preparing a batch.

2 dried red chiles
2 garlic cloves, crushed
Small piece of fresh ginger, grated
2 teaspoons black peppercorns, lightly crushed
1 blade of mace (optional)
3¾ cups white wine vinegar
12 eggs

MAKES ABOUT 3 PINTS

1 Put all the ingredients except the eggs into a nonreactive pan and bring to the boil. Lower the heat and simmer gently for 10 minutes, then remove from the heat and leave until cool. Taste the vinegar to check that it is spiced to your liking.

2 Place the eggs in a large saucepan, cover with cold water, and bring to a boil. Cover the pan, remove from the heat, and let stand for 15 minutes. Drain the eggs and cool under cold running water. Crack the shells and carefully peel the eggs, being sure to also remove the inner white skin.

3 Pack the eggs fairly loosely into the sterilized jars. Strain in the vinegar so that it covers the eggs completely and seal. Label the jars and store in a cool, dark, dry place for three to four weeks before eating. Will keep for at least six months.

Index